# Regionalism Reconsidered: The Economic Commission for Africa

## Other Titles in This Series

Apartheid and International Organizations, Richard E. Bissell

Ethnicity in Modern Africa, edited by Brian M. du Toit

Botswana: An African Growth Economy, Penelope Hartland-Thunberg

Zambia's Foreign Policy: Studies in Diplomacy and Dependence, Douglas G. Anglin and Timothy Shaw

South Africa into the 1980s, edited by Richard E. Bissell and Chester A. Crocker

Crisis in Zimbabwe, edited by Boniface Obichere

The Arab-African Connection: Political and Economic Realities, Victor T. Le Vine and Timothy W. Luke

African Upheavals Since Independence, Grace Stuart Ibingira

# Westview Special Studies on Africa

Regionalism Reconsidered:
The Economic Commission for Africa
Isebill V. Gruhn

This first in-depth study of a UN regional economic commission focuses on the Economic Commission for Africa (ECA). Concerned with both regional cooperation and integration and national institution building, Professor Gruhn studies the role of the UN system in Africa, the relationship between international development efforts and African development, and conflicting international and African trends. She concludes that neither increased self-reliance at the national level nor new global structures, although important, will eliminate the need for a coherent, realistic regional system in Africa.

Isebill V. Gruhn, associate professor of politics at the University of California, Santa Cruz, was visiting professor of African Studies at Johns Hopkins University in 1978-1979.

# Regionalism Reconsidered: The Economic Commission for Africa

Isebill V. Gruhn

Westview Press / Boulder, Colorado

*Westview Special Studies on Africa*



Published in 1979 in the United States of America by
Westview Press, Inc.
5500 Central Avenue
Boulder, Colorado 80301
Frederick A. Praeger, Publisher

Library of Congress Cataloging in Publication Data
Gruhn, Isebill V
Regionalism reconsidered.
(Westview special studies on Africa)
Bibliography: p.
Includes index.
1. Nations. Economic Commission for Africa.
2. Africa--Economic integration.
3. Regionalism--Africa. I. Title.
HC502.G78 338.96 79-5060
ISBN 0-89158-576-1

Composition for this book was provided by the author.
Printed and bound in the United States of America.

To George Lanyi and John D. Lewis
with admiration and affection

# Contents

Acknowledgements ........................... xi
Abbreviations ............................ xiii

1 INTRODUCTION ........................... 1

2 THE REGIONALIST PERSPECTIVE ............ 9

3 ECA'S ORGANIZATIONAL STRUCTURE, LEADERSHIP, STAFF AND BUDGET .......... 31

4 ECA'S ACTIVITIES AND WORK PROGRAMS ..... 67

5 REGIONALISM RECONSIDERED ............... 99

Appendix 1 - Selected African Regional and Sub-regional Organizations for Cooperation and Integration .... 137
Appendix 2 - Member States of the United Nations Economic Commission for Africa .................... 143
Appendix 3 - ECA Operational Programme 1979-1981 Sectorial Distribution .................. 145
Appendix 4 - ECA-sponsored Institutions and Their Locations ........... 146
Selected Bibliography ...................... 148
Index....................................... 152

# Acknowledgements

This study could not have been carried out without the generous and friendly reception which I received from many officials at the Economic Commission for Africa during my 1966 and 1976 visits. I am particularly indebted to Dr. T. Peter Omari whose sustained interest and helpfulness have been invaluable. Neither Dr. Omari nor other ECA officials have always shared my views on, or analysis of the Economic Commission for Africa. It has, however, been a great pleasure to discuss with them our differing perspectives.

I would also like to thank Ernst B. Haas, who helped to foster my interest in many of the matters underlying this study, for his continued interest and critical perspective on my work. My friend and colleague John Marcum contributed much through his friendship, encouragement, and substantive comments during critical times in the evolution of this study. My colleagues at Stevenson College at the University of California at Santa Cruz provided a congenial and supportive intellectual and social environment. I would like to thank the following friends who are in different fields and do not share my interest in African affairs, but who have contributed, directly and indirectly, to this study; Peter Kenez, Audrey Stanley, Ritu Prasad Meister, Robert Meister, and Alan Richards.

I am indebted to the Foreign Area Fellowship Program, which funded a one year trip to Africa in connection with a different project in 1965-66, which gave me my first introduction to the ECA. Faculty Research funds granted by the University of California, Santa Cruz, helped support my 1976 trip to Addis Ababa. This manuscript was patiently and thoughtfully edited by Lise Peterson and Benjamin Schiff who sought to rescue me from embarrassment by reviewing the manuscript in its final stage.

Finally and most importantly I would like to express my gratitude to Constance G. Anthony who, in spite of her own travels and research in Africa and pressing personal commitments, devoted endless energy both to substantively improving my work and encouraging me to complete it. I cannot imagine a more generous friend and I am much indebted to her. All of the individuals named above, and many who for reasons of space have not been mentioned, should be held responsible for the existence of this book. However, I alone am responsible for its shortcomings and errors.

Isebill V. Gruhn

Washington, D. C.
March, 1979

# Abbreviations

ADB.......African Development Bank
BCEAO.....Banque Central des Etats de l'Afrique de l'Ouest
BEAC......Banque des Etats de l'Afrique Centrale
CEAO......Communauté Economique de l'Afrique de l'Ouest
CPCM......Comité Permanet Consultatif du Magreb
EAC.......East African Community
ECA.......Economic Commission for Africa, United Nations
ECAFE.....Economic Commission for Asia and the Far East, United Nations
ECE.......Economic Commission for Europe United Nations
ECLA......Economic Commission for Latin America, United Nations
ECOSOC....Economic and Social Council, United Nations
ECOWAS....Economic Community of West African States
EFTA......European Free Trade Association
FAO.......Food and Agricultural Organization
ILO.......International Labor Organization or International Labor Office
LAFTA.....Latin American Free Trade Association
LCBC......Lake Chad Basin Commission
MULPOCs...Multi-national Programming and Operations Centers
OAS.......Organization of American States
OAU.......Organization of African Unity
OCAM......Organization Commune Africaine et Mauricienne
OMVS......Organizations pour la Mise en Valeur du Fleuve Senegal

ODEAC.....Union Douanière et Economique de l'Afrique Centrale (Central African Customs and Economic Union)
UEAC......Union des Etats de l'Afrique Central
UMOA......Union Monetaire Ouest-Africaine
UNCTAD....United Nations Conference on Trade and Development
UNDATs....United Nations International Multi-disciplinary Development Advisory Teams
UNDP......United Nations Development Program
UNESCO....United Nations Educational, Scientific and Cultural Organization
UNIDO.....United Nations Industrial Development Organization
WHO.......World Health Organization

# Regionalism Reconsidered: The Economic Commission for Africa

# 1 Introduction

The history of the United Nations Economic Commission for Africa dates back to 1946, when the UN was concerned with the reconstruction of Europe. By a resolution of the UN Economic and Social Council, a Temporary Subcommission on Economic Reconstruction of devastated areas was established on June 21 of that year. This subcommission divided itself into two working groups, one for Europe and North Africa and one for Asia and the Far East. In March of the following year the Economic and Social Council established the Economic Commission for Asia and the Far East (ECAFE), and in August it established the Economic Commission for Latin America (ECLA). In 1947 and again in 1950 resolutions were introduced with the purpose of creating an Economic Commission for North Africa and Ethiopia, but no action was taken on either occasion; many thought that the creation of such a commission was premature. Similar requests were made again in 1951 and 1956, but were turned down by the Economic and Social Council. However, the Secretariat of the United Nations was asked to study economic conditions in Africa.

The subject came up again in 1957, this time in the General Assembly. Some members argued that Africa needed an organization to collect information and expedite economic development; others claimed that Africa did not constitute a homogenous economic region. In November, 1957, a resolution of the General Assembly's Second Committee asked the Economic and Social Council to give prompt and favorable consideration to the establishment of an Economic Commission for Africa.

In accordance with that request, the Economic and Social Council, in its resolution of April 29,

1958, established the Economic Commission for Africa. Addis Ababa, Ethiopia, was selected as the site for the new Commission's headquarters, and the terms of reference for the commission were spelled out. The Economic Commission for Africa (ECA), like the UN's other regional commissions, operates under the general supervision of the Economic and Social Council and of the General Assembly. The terms of reference of the ECA require that the Commission initiate and participate in measures for facilitating concerted action to relieve the economic and technological problems of Africa; that it make or sponsor investigations into economic and technological problems and development; that it undertake or sponsor the collection, evaluation, and dissemination of economic, technological, and statistical information; that it perform such advisory services as countries of the region may desire, provided that these do not overlap with those provided by other bodies of the UN or by its specialized agencies, and that it assist the Economic and Social Council, at its request, in discharging its functions within the region in connection with any economic problems including those in the field of technical assistance; that it assist in the development of coordinated policies for promoting economic and technological development in the region; and that it deal, where appropriate, with the social aspects of economic development and with the relationship between economic and social factors.[1]

The terms of reference for the UN's Regional Commissions assign a dual mandate to each one: act as part of the UN's international structure, but serve the special needs of the specific region. A Regional Commission is intended to assist the Economic and Social Council of the United Nations in discharging its functions; at the same time, it is intended to serve its clients within the region and to help formulate policies for regional economic and social development. Obviously a Regional Commission may choose either to adopt, or seek to overcome this potential split personality. The charge of the Regional Commissions is sufficiently vague to allow each one to define its own personality, and to reflect the special needs of each region. But the dual mandate has forced each Regional Commission to make conscious choices between, or else seek to integrate, potentially conflicting demands--those from the international structure of which it is a part, and those from the region it was established to serve.

The Economic Commission for Africa has developed its institutional structure without resolving this contradiction. Since its inception in 1958, the ECA has been one of the dominant forces for regional cooperation and integration[2] on the African continent. The ECA has both mirrored prevalent regionalist ideologies and theories and contributed its own interpretations. It has served as a midwife for the building of inter-state institutions, lobbying in Africa and abroad in support of this effort. The ECA has not been merely an African regional mechanism, but has operated as an integral component of the United Nations' machinery as well. In this role it participated in the UN's early efforts to diagnose African development problems and assist in their remedy. Its unique contribution to this effort was to translate the aspirations of the regionalists into developmental vocabulary. In Africa the two goals were intimately linked from the very start.

Perhaps the most important lesson of the two decades in which most of Africa gained political independence was that assumptions made about the speed with which economic growth and modernization would take place were not very realistic. Academic theorists shared with African ideologues like Nkrumah the belief that the very newness of the African states allowed for some circumvention of the paraphenalia of sovereignty and nationalism that constituted the historically-inherited obstacles to the uniting of Europe. The European sovereign states, jealous of their identities, required ingenious integration processes to achieve cooperation and unity. But in Africa, it was supposed, new states artifically created through colonial administration could more easily avoid schisms. Indeed, theorists and ideologues argued that continental unity and regional integration in Africa would serve to prevent the rise of nationalism.

But in fact, the past twenty years of African experience indicate the presence of more, rather than fewer, obstacles to integration than in Europe. The rockiness of the road travelled by the many inter-African organizations has many and varied explanations. I believe, however, that some simple categories might help identify the main sources of difficulty these organizations faced in trying to foster regional integration in Africa.

## NATIONALISM AND THE SOVEREIGNTY OF STATES

It was a miscalculation on the part of ideologues to assume that national independence movements, which after achievement of political independence concerned themselves largely with the search for national identities, would produce good candidates for collective problem-solving. It is not surprising, in historical retrospect, that the leadership emerging out of the national movements was not keen on divesting itself of its newly-acquired authoritiy. The failure of the Mali Federation[5] showed that even contiguous territories with the same colonial heritage found it difficult to join national interests in a single union; the forfeiture of national decision-making in favor of collective decision-making was not facilitated by the newness of the states.

## LOW LEVEL OF INTERSTATE INFRASTRUCTURE AND TRANSACTIONS

Attempts at integrating the affairs of states with differing colonial heritages added obstacles of language and the lack of similar political and economic infrastructures. The colonial period had formed political and economic entities with few structural links between them. Most African countries had economies that were competitive with, rather than complementary to, those of their neighbors; they used different bureaucratic practices, different accounting systems, different monetary zones.

Theories of integration had focused on institutions of trade, such as customs unions and common markets, as starting points for African integration. But customs unions and common markets make sense only if inter-state trade in a region already exists and constitutes a respectable percentage of the total trade--as it did in Western Europe. In sub-Sahara Africa, however, trade among neighboring states frequently amounted to no more than 4% of the total trade. In the colonial era, African countries had consciously been structured for trade with metropole countries and other industrial states; it is thus not surprising that contiguous states whose primary export commodities were the same (e.g., ground nuts, cocoa) could in the 1960s perceive very little self-interest in copying Europe's free trade areas and common markets.

In addition, most African states had been left with communication and transportation infrastructures that served their economic structures: railways and roads ran from the inland areas to ports, rather than connecting cities and neighboring states, and telecommunications linked African capitals with Paris and London (communicating with a neighboring state frequently required going through a European exchange). Thus the infrastructure, so far as it was developed at all, serviced overseas links rather than interstate ones, and tended to exacerbate the problem of integrating African economies.

## INTERNATIONAL DEPENDENCE

The links with metropoles were, after political independence, transformed into bilateral relationships to the detriment of inter-African relationships--especially those crossing former colonial boundaries. It is worth noting that while post-WWII Europe was similarly dependent on the US, regional integration was still fostered, not hindered, since the US was strongly supportive in word and action of the European Economic Community. In contrast, European metropole countries, even when verbally in favor of African regional integration, undermined the process by cultivating bilateral trade and aid links.

The usual life-cycle of an inter-African organization started with a series of inter-state conferences, which culminated in a charter-signing ceremony attended by heads of states, and the selection of a headquarters site. This was followed by the creation of an organizational bureaucracy, which then generally encountered financial difficulties, bureaucratic disarray, loss of interest by the organization's membership, and decline (and sometimes demise) of the organization. It has become a common observation that many inter-African organizations are merely 'paper organizations'; that in spite of all the preparatory activities, the high levels of politicization at founding conferences, and the pledges of support from several states, they either failed to materialize at all, or else their intended development and functions never progressed beyond the establishment of a nuclear bureaucracy too ill-equipped, staffed, and funded to carry on even minimal tasks. Many of the reasons for these failures will be discussed in subsequent chapters; suffice it to say here that the political climate, the lack of resolve on the part of the organization's membership, and the shortage of financial and human resources explain at least partially why there are so many moribund organizatons in Africa during the past two decades.

The reasons for this are important. Post-independence states lacked national leaders who either perceived or were able to politically acknowledge the fact that national, and indeed regional, development could proceed incrementally. Indeed, one might argue that national decision-makers frequently convinced themselves that rapid economic change would come about as a result of the marshalling of political commitment. Regional agreements were thus made on totally unrealistic bases: a group of several African states, with only skeletal staffs and miniscule budgets sought to make up for the lack of an inter-state infrastructure, and sought to produce instant benefits. When these benefits for member states were not forthcoming, political actors lost interest. Political impatience exacerbated the deeply-rooted problems faced by African regional integration, and undercut the possibilities for newly founded institutions to incrementally develop their capabilities.

There is little question that the 1960s were turbulent years both for the ideas and for the institutional manifestations surrounding regional cooperation and regional integration. The complexity of the organizational map (see Appendix I) and the very uneven development and organizational capacity of so many institutions contributed to a general sense of frustration regarding regionalism in Africa. New, untried regional structures were developed and were in turn confronted with the overwhelming problems of the development needs of the African continent. African leadership, disillusioned with the promise of regionalism, joined in the international call for a complete restructuring of international economic relationships to serve the development needs of Third World states. However, this ideological shift masked the on-going pragmatic commitment of many African states to the institutional survivors of the first era of African regional development. It could in fact be argued that at the very time when political rhetoric indicates the demise of regionalism, the actual management of African inter-state cooperation and the utilization of regional and subregional institutions for economic and social development is at an all time high. African leaders no longer perceive regionalism as *the* answer to development obstacles, but do view it *as* an essential component of an effective strategy to that end. Aid, capital investment, technology transfer and all other varieties of pump-priming resource transfers between industrial and African states will fail to accomplish desired growth and development as long as African institutional capabilities are weak. The regional alternative, while no longer the subject of political polemic, is alive and well, and the ECA has made a major contribution to keeping it alive.

At its core this is a study of African institution-building. The following chapters will examine the ideas and theories which promoted it, the evolution of structure and capability, the articulation of development programs and projects and the international context of competition and judgment. The ECA is a complex international organization and is not easily accounted for as either a regional or a global institution. As we will see, its position between two sets of institutional objectives and capabilities is responsible both for the innovativeness of its contribution to African regional institution-building and for its morass of irrelevant administrative and programatic commitments. However, its pursuit of strategies of regional development and inter-state institution-building has survived not only early, conspicuous failures but also its tortured attempt to resolve a contradictory institutional mandate.

NOTES

1. UN Document, E/CN.14/424, United Nations Economic Commissions, pp. 3-4.

2. The word 'integration' whenever it is used in this study is intended to refer to the process whereby states transfer authority to an inter-state institution.

3. For a good discussion of the evolution and demise of the Mali Federation, see William J. Foltz, _From French West Africa to the Mali Federation_, New Haven: Yale Univ. Press, 1965. Foltz' book is not only useful for an understanding of the ill-fated Mali Federation, but as an illustrative case study of the difficulties facing attempted African unification efforts in the post colonial era.

# 2 The Regionalist Perspective

## Early Ideologies and Theorists

The political imperative of African unity was a theme that dominated the thought of some of the more radical post-independence leaders. Among them, the name Kwame Nkrumah is a name most easily identified as advocating continental unity, not merely as a means of overcoming poverty and speeding industrialization, but as a means of achieving independence from neo-colonial incursions and gaining leverage in the international arena.[1] Other African leaders--Julius Nyerere[2] among the more radical, or Houphouet-Boigny among the more moderate--favored African unity, but saw sub-regional arrangements as the first steps toward economic development and political leverage.

Because much of the 1960s' discussion on the economic and political issues of unification was carried on in Western academic literature, it is sometimes forgotten that African leaders were often at the forefront of these discussions--and their outlooks were no more uniform than those of scholars writing from greater physical and spiritual distances.

## Leopold Senghor

One of the early voices addressing the issue of African unity was that of Leopold Senghor, Senegalese statesman and poet. Senghor, along with other black intellectuals such as Aime Cesaire (Martinique), made up a literary-cultural-philosophic circle in Paris in the 1930s. In 1934 Senghor and Cesaire founded a journal, L'Etudiant

*Noir*, in which they set out their literary conception of Negritude. Negritude was defined as "the consciousness of being black"; it stressed, in evocative terms, all that was African. Black womanhood, the glory of the African landscape, and a tendency to reject modern civilization were ongoing themes in the poetry and prose published in *L'Etudiant Noir*. Senghor's own poetry is an affirmation of the black self in the face of Western civilization. The themes of Negritude continued to be developed by French-speaking Black intellectuals throughout the 1940s and '50s while great political changes were taking place in Africa.[3]

Negritude did not merely suggest that "Black is Beautiful," but also that being black transcended tribal and national differences. According to Senghor, what Negritude is all about is "the cultural heritage, the values, and above all the spirit of black civilization."[4] For Senghor, the common racial and cultural denominator could serve as the cement and building blocks for economic and political unification or integration of Africa. But the concrete realities of post-independence Africa were to prove that Senghor's evocation of Negritude as the basis for African unity was to remain a literary achievement of the Negritude writers. Senghor's own country, Senegal, participated (under Senghor's leadership) in the ill-fated Mali Federation in the early '60s. The failure of even two former colonies to work together must have suggested quite early on even to Senghor and his sympathizers, that racial brotherhood would prove inadequate to overcoming indigenous and colonially-wrought schisms in Africa in the post-independence decade.[5]

Nevertheless, the concept of Negritude, with its effort to call attention to the racial, cultural, and historical links among Africans, was an important theme in the discussion about African unity and integration. Senghor's forty-year international reputation as a poet and statesman and his enthusiasm for maintaining Eurafrican links, especially in the economic realm, have won for Negritude a great deal of international attention. It is probably not an exaggeration to say that many Western thinkers in the 1950s and '60s assumed that, if economic and political barriers could be overcome in Africa, the roots for African Unity described in Senghor's writings probably did exist.

## Kwame Nkrumah and Other Pan-Africanists

Pan Africanism is a difficult term to define with any precision. Like Negritude, Pan Africanism predates African independence by several decades. Like Negritude, it was (and is) a movement of Africans and Afro-Americans. The two share many themes: in a sense, Negritude could be considered a sub-species of Pan Africanism. However, because Negritude became identified with French speakers, and Pan Africanism largely with English speakers, and because one emphasized cultural factors while the other emphasized political ones, Negritude and Pan Africanism are often seen as competing rather than complementary forces in African unification politics. The history and complexities of Pan Africanism[6] will not be discussed here. However, the influence of Pan Africanist thinking on post-independence politics is of direct interest in an examination of African attitudes about unity and integration.

The thinking of Kwame Nkrumah, Ghana's nationalist leader and first head of state, dominated the conceptualization of Pan Africanism in the 1950s and early '60s. His ideas have developed over a period of two decades before African independence while he was a participant in Pan Africanist meetings in England and Africa. Nkrumah argued for African unity less in terms of racial and cultural foundations than in terms of political and economic necessity. Much of Nkrumah's attention was directed, often at the expense of the short-term interest of his own country, at organizing for a United States of Africa. To underline independent Ghana's link with Pan Africanism, Nkrumah brought West Indian leader and Pan Africanist George Padmore to Ghana in 1958. After Padmore's death the following year Nkrumah claimed leadership of the Pan Africanist movement.

When about half the continent attained political independence in 1960, the establishment of so many small and seemingly unviable states, along with their tendency to quickly form blocs, made it clear that Pan Africanist ideals could not provide the foundation for continental unity.[7] The Organization of African Unity, founded in 1963 under the aegis of conservative Ethiopia, was a far cry from Nkrumah's vision of "union government for Africa"; it was perceived as a compromise--a means of creating a minimal foundation upon which African unity could someday be based.

By 1966, when Nkrumah was deposed as Ghana's head of state, Pan Africanism and African unity were generally seen as distant goals, and Nkrumah was suspected of putting forth his United States of Africa (with himself as its first president) as a matter of personal ambition.

Being firmly committed to continental unification, Nkrumah was opposed to more limited regional arrangements, such as the Mali Federation (Senegal and Mali) or the East African Community (Kenya, Uganda, and Tanzania). Nkrumah saw regional integration efforts as yet another form of balkanization. This view brought him into conflict with other African leaders and with external advocates of regional integration and cooperation.

Julius Nyerere, Tanzania's nationalist leader and first head of state, was also an early and strong advocate of African unity and was a supporter of the OAU. At the same time, however, he was staunchly committed to the East African Common Market and Common Services Organization. Unlike Nkrumah, he did not see subregional arrangements as an impediment to African unity. Nyerere said in 1967 that "Africa is one but it is also thirty-eight and more. Only a recognition of this fact, and its limitations, will allow progress . . . Unity will be hard to attain."[8]

Modibo Keita, the leader of Mali, remarked as early as 1960 that "the mystical force of African unity is not yet strong enough to bring African states together. Only events will do this by putting pressure on African leaders who, by a reaction of self-defense, will all join hands."[9] By the mid-sixties, neither events, nor the feeble OAU, nor efforts to develop a continental consciousness provided a rallying point for African unity. Idealism of the kind exhibited by Senghor and Nkrumah--idealism that sought to provide for Africa an identity independent from its colonial heritage--found its greatest support in the pre- and early post-independence years. The complexities of forging economic and political unity among African states came into sharper focus only after the euphoria of independence wore off.

By the end of the 1960s both international observers and African leaders began to look at

European experiences with the Common Market and the Free Trade Association for guidance in small state management. Many thought that Africa could foster regional integration through the establishment of similar economic and technical mechanisms. One of Kwame Nkrumah's countrymen, Robert Gardiner, who headed the UN's Regional Economic Commission for Africa (ECA), was a strong advocate of African regional arrangements leading to multistate integration.[10] As the unfeasibility of continental unification along either cultural or political lines became apparent, the impetus to organize regional or subregional groups along political, economic, linguistic or geographic lines increased. By the second half of the '60s, calls for regional integration tended to drown out those few voices still urging African unity.

## The View of Theorists in the Post-independence Era

Much of the academic discussion during the '60s regarding African unity and regional integration was written by Western European and North American authors. East European and Soviet scholarly activity was relatively barren during this period.[11] African contributions were limited, by and large, to the speeches and writings of the political figures cited earlier.

Among the Western scholars who were not of Marxist persuasion, few could be found who believed that either Negritude or Pan Africanism would soon lead to African unification; Western scholarly literature tended to focus on more limited subregional integration and/or cooperation. To young economists and political scientists interested in African affairs, studies of post-WWII European reconstruction lent the hope that regional integration could be applicable to the African context. It would be accurate, therefore, to say that theorizing on the part of Western scholars about African regional integration was at least partially induced by contemporary fashion rather than by intimate acquaintance with African circumstances.

It might be useful at this point to differentiate between the terms "regional cooperation" and "regional integration." Regional cooperation is a vague term, applicable to any inter-state activity with less than universal participation designed to meet some common need. The term regional integration has acquired several quite technical definitions, but when used in this study will refer either to the process or the achieved reality of national units coming to share part or all of their decision-making authority with an emerging international institution.[12] It should be further noted that when the term regional integration is applied to Africa in the scholarly literature it almost always assumes that 'region' refers not to the entire continent but to subregions thereof.

Ernst Haas, a central figure in the neo-functionalist school of regional integration theorists, based his own early work on an analysis of Europe.[13] Haas was concerned with "explanations of how and why states cease to be wholly sovereign, how and why they voluntarily mingle, merge, and mix with their neighbors so as to lose the factual attributes of sovereignty while acquiring new techniques for resolving conflict between themselves."[14] Haas' work on Europe and the subsequent theoretical refinements of functional integration in his book <u>Beyond the Nation-State</u>[15] served as take-off points for much descriptive work on Africa.

By the middle '60s Haas himself had begun to apply his understandings to non-European contexts.[16] Constantly attentive to refinements of his own work, he was by the '70s issuing warnings to those who had developed a tendency to misapply or misinterpret regional integration theorizing: "Regional cooperation, organization, and systems and subsystems may help describe steps along the way; but they should not be confused with resulting conditions."[17]

What Haas was responding to was a tendency among students of regional integration to confuse the end state of an integrated community with the process of integration. The policies and institutional arrangements which Haas referred to as "steps along the way" were frequently written about as if they themselves were the end result. Haas perceived multi- and unifunctional organizations as <u>means</u> of habituating national actors to "sharing part or all of their authority." The normative <u>aim</u> was the development of new political communities wherein individual states shared their sovereignty with an international organization. The success or failure of an integration process would therefore be measured by the extent to which a transfer of authority from individual states to common institutions had taken place.

Of course, whether the integration process is perceived of as leading to the goal or as constituting the goal itself, the same consequences can result. That is, states will either way come to share individual authority with a collective mechanism. Thus, confusion of 'steps along the way' with the goal--i.e., confusing the proces with the achievement of integration--may be quibbling if the unintended consequence of the process is that integration takes place.

In reality, integration theorizing about Africa ran into more serious difficulties than confusions of process and goal, or of intended and unintended consequences. Throughout the '60s, as the number of regional integration studies on Africa increased, almost all aspects of the African situation were found to be at variance with those in Europe. The actors were different, their goals were different, the role of exogenous variables was different--to name only the most obvious.[18] Nevertheless, the belief persisted that African variations could either be accounted for by the theory through the addition of some variables, and the re-emphasis of others, or could, with some adjustments, be made to explain and predict the likelihood of failure of subregional arrangements.[19]

Karl Deutsch and his followers (generally known as the Transactionalists),[20] also theorized from the standpoint of an understanding of European history. They argued that the reduction of conflict and the development of community was to be achieved through increased transactions between private and public persons of different societies. In these terms, maintaining colonially-inherited links of language and custom, in addition to developing post-independence links, would lead to African unity. Transactionalist thinking was thus not in conflict with regional integration theorizing in any serious way, and was generally supportive of all inter-African cooperation and/or integration. Given the size and development of the African continent, however, it can easily be seen that a rapid increase in interstate transactions was unlikely. Possibly because they appeared less promising as quick remedies for

African ills, Transactionalist ideas were adopted by few scholars of African affairs. However, less-theoretically-inclined descriptive scholars echoed Transactionalist calls for inter-African cooperative organizations, multi-state conferences, preservation of language groupings, etc. (In a real sense the Transactionalists made a link with Negritude in that racial, cultural and linguistic identities could be cultivated across national borders.)

The criticism, frequently heard in the 1960s, that African leaders were spending too much time attending inter-African conferences was countered by Transactionalist observers, who suggested that discussions among African leaders at conferences was an essential ingredient of regional economic and political institution-building. But in spite of these infusions of Transactionalist thinking into the African context, Transactionalism played a rather low-key role in scholarly circles concerned with African affairs and, unlike African Unification or Regional Integration, did not engage the interest of dominant African leaders.

## The Marxist Perspective

Western Marxist scholarly writings during the '50s and '60s were not consistent in their theory or criticism on the issues under consideration here. At first, there was a general inclination to support (using both the cultural arguments of the Negritude writers and the political/historical arguments of the Pan Africanists) Nkrumah's call for a United States of Africa. Only African Unity, Marxists argued, could produce genuine independence from capitalistic neo-colonial forces.[21] Unlike Nkrumah, however, Marxist analysts sometimes advocated subregional integration as a means to achieve economic development and eventual continental unification. Interestingly, Marxist support of regional arrangements expressed itself rather negatively: Marxists charged that in Western industrial states the neo-colonial policy of dealing with African states through balkanizing, and bilateral relationships was undermining African regional integration efforts.[22]

Western Marxist scholars, while generally opposing the European common market itself, joined their non-Marxist counterparts, by using the European Common Market as their empirical and theoretical starting point, but used it in a dual sense. On the one hand, the EEC was seen as a potential workable model for Africa, a way of developing economic and political unity, and thus winning independence from Western domination. On the other hand, the Common Market itself was perceived of as a threat to African development because it enabled Europe to exert more neocolonial pressure on Africa.[23] (On this latter point Western Marxist analysis concurred with Nkrumah's views.) Marxist analysis underwent some changes in the '70s; this phase will be dealt with later in this chapter.

Western Marxists in the first two post-independence decades tended, then, to share the widespread optimistic belief that rapid economic growth was feasible in Africa, provided balkanization could be countered, regional integration fostered, and progress towards continental unity achieved. Like other Western scholars, Marxists believed that lessons learned in Europe could be applied to Africa.

Scholars of all the theoretical persuasions discussed above have increasingly come to find that basing their theorizing on European experiences and Western understandings has adversely affected their explanatory and predictive powers. While many committed regionalists have concluded that the politics of African integration could best be understood from the vantage point of a deeper comprehension of African circumstances, contemporary theorizing on African interstate cooperation has been reoriented to a new level of analysis.

## Current African Attitudes and Theorists

During the '60s, regional integration theorists concerned with Africa sought to adjust their theories both in their applicability to Europe and their transferability to Africa. Exchanges of information between students of African integration and students of European integration brought to the integration literature further refinements of the understanding of differences between industrial and non-industrial states. At the same time, events in Africa made it clear that this issue was no longer one of preventing balkanization: that had already taken place. Rather it was one of understanding why, after a decade of independence, instead of development and integration, economic stagnation and political chaos had taken place.

The writings of students of African affairs reflected the deflation of euphoria among Africans themselves.[24] A more realistic examination of African circumstances began to appear in studies of the African situation. Factors such as manpower shortages, the embryonic state of national and interstate infrastructures, and the extent to which forces external to Africa were affecting its development all began to be taken more seriously. It will be shown later in this study that the ECA itself played a considerable role by calling attention to African realities, by helping to establish a regional institutional structure and by guiding human and financial resources into areas of newly identified priorities.

## Changing (Neo-Functional) Perspectives

In 1975 Ernst Haas wrote that the "problems to which regional unification was thought to be a solution are not in fact regional in scope" and that in Africa the "political imperatives of state- and nation-building are of such a magnitude as to make regional collective action seem beside the point."[25] Certainly the track record of African regional arrangements is so poor as to suggest his conclusions are accurate. However, it seems ironic that while international attention is being drawn away from regional efforts in Africa, and towards the larger international arena (or on single-country development within the context of an international structure), the number of regional arrangements on the African continent is continuing to grow.

Haas' notion of 'incrementalism' is one of the key factors in the disjunction between neo-functionalist theorizing and African realities of the past 20 years. Incrementalism--described as "a decision-making process, a routine for collectively coping with problems in such a manner as to let new decisions emerge piecemeal from inadequately-made prior decisions, only to be supplemented later with another set of piecemeal decisions"--is how theorists envisioned regional integration proceeding, both in Africa and elsewhere.[26] I think it is accurate to say that it is "doubtful that African organizations have ever acted in accord with the 'assumption' (of incrementalism)"; it seems equally correct to question whether "the pattern of action implicit in the interregional efforts of various groupings of late-developing and non-aligned states to reorder the values of the world economy is consistent with incrementalism."[27]

Even Haas is today careful to differentiate, in his most recent writings, between European and 'late-developing' countries. This differentiation is based in part on the degree to which regional integration--as explanatory and normative theory or as policy and practice--has become obsolete in a given area. His 'degrees of obsolescence' aside, Haas appears to feel that if the theoretical focus on regional integration is _not_ obsolete, it ought to be. This does not mean that he ignores the efforts of 'late-developing' countries to take collective action in their struggles for survival and advancement: he says that the objectives of collective action always are

> _at first_--the intensification of the economic development process by means of a free trade area or a common market, or through the creation of some common technical or administrative services. This results in the ubiquitous 'equity' or 'distribution' crises in such unions. The participants come to the conclusion that growth will be distributed unevenly among the members, with the initially wealthiest members reaping disproportionate benefits. Externalization now appears in the guise of the _dependencia_ doctrine: the members decide that they cannot obtain the right kind of economic growth unless they make a common front vis-a-vis their major customers and suppliers of investment capital. Hence they attempt to transform their union into a collective arrangement which gives them a common industrialization plan, a common investment policy, a common legal code with respect to the treatment of foreign investors (including restrictions on investors), and a common negotiating stance with respect to agreements governing the exportation of primary products.[28]

Haas concludes, correctly I believe, that when these activities do not produce the desired results (specifically, I might add, when development is not as rapid as was hoped) an attempt is made to shift the blame to an external target. Still, the actors themselves have concluded that forces outside the region or subregion are in fact the central obstacles to development.

Contemporary theorists, as I have noted earlier, have begun to emphasize the fact that international economic interdependence is such that neither national development nor regional integration addresses many of the problems that ultimately impede the progress of national development and regional integration. Haas also feels that this conclusion is accurate as it applies to Western Europe--hence the Obsolescence of Regional Integration Theory--because "matters transcend the space and the jurisdiction of the Community's institutions because they are functions of economic interdependence with trading partners outside of Europe."[29] He also finds that "efforts to cope through collective action are channeled into other international organizations and forums as well as into bilateral arrangements."[30] However, Haas seems less certain what a similar recognition on the part of the 'late-developing' countries signifies. On the one hand, when late-developing countries argue that the cause of their slow development should be looked for beyond the boundaries of a state or a regional community, they are making demands on the industrial world, not just describing the way certain issues transcend community boundaries. On the other hand, the fact that late-developing states have organized collectively to make demands of the wider international system suggests to Haas (and to others) that if and when some demands are met, this may in itself undermine collective action, since new interdependency relationships will be formed across regional boundaries.[31] In short, the late-developing states too will join the ranks of those who no longer believe in the efficacy of regional integration.

## The Decline of the Regionalist Perspective and The New Emphasis on a New International Economic Order

Political actors, as well as those writing in scholarly journals who concern themselves with the finer points of theories (and the appropriate variables and indicators to accompany the theories), both see much concrete evidence for the decreasing relevance of regional integration. The consistent failures of various regional integration efforts--the recent demise of the East African Community, for example--serve as testimony to the obstacles faced by regional integration. In addition, events of the 1970s have made certain issues increasingly salient at the international-system level; theorists and actors alike have come to view sustained economic growth for the industrial countries and accelerated economic development for the late-developing countries as matters of universal interest. A new set of ideas has begun to claim more attention than those of regional integration.

The phrase New International Economic Order, having for some time dominated political addresses, calls for action, and international negotiations, has now come to dominate scholarly activity. The then somewhat radical notions of Raul Prebisch and his associates of the 1950s and 1960s (who, in seeing international structural reasons for underdevelopment, had much in common with Marxists) have been assimilated by mainstream intellectual fashions of today. The notion of inter-dependence and the search for systemic solutions to the discrepancy between industrial and non-industrial states are becoming more popular than theorizing about regional integration.

The entrance of this international systemic focus into mainstream development thinking probably took place during discussions of the Strategies for the Second UN Development Decade, which were adopted by the General Assembly in 1970 and reviewed in 1973. The Strategies themselves mention only in passing, however, the need for international structural changes, and the LDCs were no doubt correct in their belief that the UN had little ability to produce serious changes. The crucial point, for actors and observers alike, was the OPEC oil embargo in 1973. In spite of the obvious singularity of the oil producers' ability to bring the industrial world to heel--peanut and banana growers could not realistically expect to exert similar leverage--the jarring effect of the OPEC initiative was to lend a new sense of urgency and respectability to a number of notions that heretofore have been seen as the preserve of a certain group of radicals.

As a result of the oil and energy crises of 1973 the UN held, in March and April of the following year, a Sixth Special Session of the General Assembly[32] on the subject of raw materials and development. Out of the Sixth Special Session there emerged a code of conduct for economic relations, called the Charter of Economic Rights and Duties of States,[33] which had been under discussion at UNCTAD since 1972 but which was now given a prominent place in the deliberations of the General Assembly. OPEC and the non-oil-producing LDCs maintained a coalition throughout 1974 and 1975 that made more visible the LDCs and their demands for greater equity within the international economic system. By mid-1975 the industrial countries were understanding the similarities between oil and the other raw materials provided by LDCs. The industrial countries, including the US, were beginning to see that the differences between raw-material producers and consumers were closely related to the relationship between developed and developing countries.[34]

In 1975, just before its regular Autumn session, the General Assembly held a Special Seventh Session[35] devoted to development and international economic cooperation. While the convening of this session was not meant to indicate a promise that international structural changes would be undertaken in the near future, or even to indicate the UN's agreement that such changes should take place, it was at least an acknowledgment, on the part of the industrial states, that the LDCs were asking for structural changes (not remedial tinkering) and that the industrial states could no longer avoid negotiating with them. The general theme of the NIEO has continued to dominate the meetings of UN specialized agencies since then. The UNEP conference in April, 1976 in Nairobi, and even more importantly, the UNCTAD IV conference held the following month, considered the general idea of structural changes in the international economic system, and also came up with some specific demands. That year's conferences of the ILO, FAO, and other UN agencies also addressed the subject of international structural changes.

In addition to keeping the subject alive at these global membership conferences, proponents of the NIEO made it the focus of 18 months of negotiations at the Conference on International Economic Cooperation--often referred to as the North-South Dialogue--held in Paris during 1976 and 1977. The following countries were represented in the Dialogue:

| The group of eight (North) | | The group of nineteen (South) | |
|---|---|---|---|
| Australia | USA | Algeria | Mexico |
| Canada | Japan | Saudi Arabia | Nigeria |
| EEC | Sweden | Argentina | Pakistan |
| Spain | Switzerland | Brazil | Peru |
| | | Cameroon | Egypt |
| | | India | Venezuela |
| | | Indonesia | Yugoslavia |
| | | Iraq | Zaire |
| | | Iran | Zambia |
| | | Jamaica | |

The LDCs' main demands during the dialogue were for

a substantial increase in the volume of aid, technology transfers, and assistance to agricultural development; a 0.7% of GNP transfer, preferential treatment of LDC exports, and regulations governing transnational companies;

a moratorium on all repayment of debts;

investment funds for the development of their own energy resources;

an integrated program protecting their earnings from the export of their basic commodities; and

reform of the International Monetary Fund, including bigger quotas and increased voting rights for LDCs, plus special drawing rights and more flexible conditions for borrowing.[36]

As one can imagine, many of these demands have not been met, although the industrial states continue to express their willingness to discuss these matters.

I should add that scholars have begun to take note of these developments. Many issues are being examined from an international systemic viewpoint.[37] The OPEC scare called attention to a range of resources well-suited to international management and to environmental issues that transcend national and regional boundaries--to name only two of the most obvious of the issues that engage theorists and policy-makers alike. Just as the most widespread post-WWII notion was that regional integration could solve the economic problems of both industrial and non-industrial states, so today the notion is widespread that many of the problems facing mankind, including those of accelerated development of the 'late-developing' states, need to be studied and solved on a systemic basis. The catch-phrase "New International Economic Order' is less a description of a new reality than it is a call to arms for theorists and policy-makers--it is a reality only in that the call to arms has so far had some measure of success.

## The Changing Marxist Position

In recent years Marxist thinking has also undergone changes in its explanation for the failure of inter-African institution-building. It will be recalled that Western Marxists favored African regional integration in the '60s, echoing many of the descriptive explanations of non-Marxist neo-functional integration theorists. While functional integration theorists explained subsequent failures on the basis of African over-politicization of functional efforts and on the lack of patience with incrementalism, Marxist analysis tended to blame them on the interference of Western capitalistic states. But while the explanations for difficulties and failures thus differed, the advocacy for regional integration as a normative goal remained the same.

In the 1970s, however, Marxists revised their position, and today African regional integration and cooperation schemes (such as common markets) are seen as reflecting the interests of African elites who are doing the bidding of foreign capitalistic elites--at the expense of national development and self-reliance for the majority of the African population. As can be seen, the Marxist interpretation moved from advocating integration, and accusing the industrial countries of fostering balkanization, to claiming that integration is a ploy on the part of Western nations to generate profit.[38]

Contemporary Marxist writing tends to advocate African national self-reliance and argues against inter-African institutional development for the reasons mentioned above. Presumably there is nothing in the Marxist position that would oppose continental unification, could it be willed into existence. But the links between African states in the way of common markets, currency regions, and other developments easing commerce and trade are mainly contrary to current Marxists prescriptions for the African continent.

It seems to me that the Marxists are accurate in their observation that the industrial states and multinational corporations are gaining benefits from the development of inter-African cooperation, increases in market size and investment possibilities, and the creation of banking and currency mechanisms. However, institutions like common markets can be used to a variety of ends, and there appears nothing inherent in these mechanisms themselves that suggests that justice and equity within or among states automatically flows from, or is automatically precluded by, regional arrangements. Institutions that ease regional and international relations are empty structures; the social and economic priorities of a state or states give them content. Alliances with varying degrees of cooperative institution-building have at times served to strengthen members against external threats, and at other times have invited external forces to annex and control them. The notion that inter-African cooperation can potentially lead to strengthen Africa politically and economically is not necessarily negated by citing evidence that particular institutions have served, or are serving to perpetuate inequalities within a region, or are fostering dependency relationships between the members of the arrangement and external forces.

## Conclusion

Both the antagonism towards regionalism on the part of Marxist writers and the increasing disinterest in regionalism on the part of non-Marxist writers are based on examinations of the same historical data. Both realize the failures of regional integration, as theory and as process; both are seeking to explain these failures. For Marxists, the international economic structure, which allows neo-colonialism to occur, is to blame for the sluggishness of African economic development and political decay. For non-Marxists, political and economic corruption, a tendency to overpoliticize issues best left to technically competent experts, and an unwillingness to employ incremental processes are key explanations for failure. Both types of observer blame international economic and political factors for the malfunctioning of African regionalism. Both tend to assume that global restructuring is necessary to solve the problems: the Marxists because such restructuring would create a more equitable international economy and help to overthrow the indigenous capitalist elite in Africa, and the non-Marxists because it would lead to greater capital transfers to disadvantaged African states.

What tends to be dealt with inadequately in both types of analysis is the fact that resource transfers do not produce development unless institutions exist, manpower is available, and infrastructures are developed to convert capital into human welfare and societal development. Much theorizing about regional cooperation and integration, and now about international economic restructuring, has tended to underemphasize these requirements, to the detriment of the explanatory and prescriptive power of the theories.

The thesis of this study is that African regional arrangements are today relevant in a way that they have not been in the past, and that they are important in precisely the area of converting capital resources into human welfare and societal development. African regional arrangements are needed as supplements, rather than alternatives, to an NIEO. Post World-War-II regional integration theorizing may be dead, but regional institutions on the African continent are only now coming of age.

The chapters which follow focus upon the Economic Commission for Africa. My examination of two decades of ECA operations is intended to accomplish two separate goals. First, to consider the ECA in light of its own critical contributions to the formulation of regionalist theory and practice. Second, to indicate what, if any role ECA might play in the contemporary context.

The first task is to describe ECA's organizational structure, placing an emphasis on leadership, staff and budget.

NOTES

1. See Kwame Nkrumah Ghana, The Autobiography of Kwame Nkrumah, Edinburgh: Thomas Nelson and Sons, 1957.

_________, I Speak of Freedom, London: Heinemann, 1961.

_________, Africa Must Unite, New York: Praeger, 1963.

2. Julius Nyerere, "A United States of Africa," Journal of Modern African Studies, Vol. 1, 1963. See also Joseph S. Nye, Jr., Pan Africanism and East African Integration, Cambridge, Mass.: Harvard Univ. Press, 1965, Chapter VI, for a discussion of Nyerere's support of an East African Federation.

3. For a good discussion of the central themes of Negritude and the relationship of Negritude to Pan Africanism in general, see Immanuel Geiss, The Pan African Movement, New York: Africana Publishing Co., 1974, Chapter 15.

4. Quoted in Jacques Maquet, Africanity: The Cultural Unity of Black Africa, London: Oxford Univ. Press, 1972, p. 7.

5. For a good discussion of the evolution and demise of the Mali Federation, see William J. Foltz, From French West Africa to the Mali Federation, New Haven: Yale Univ. Press, 1965. Foltz' book is not only useful for an understanding of the ill-fated Mali Federation, but as an illustrative case study of the difficulties facing attempted African unification efforts in the past colonial era.

6 . For a detailed history of Pan African, see Immanuel Geiss, The Pan African Movement, op. cit. See also Colin Legum, Pan Africanism: a Short Political Guide, New York: Praeger, 1962: Robert Chrisman and Nathan Hare, eds., Pan Africanism, New York: Bobbs-Merrill Company, 1974.

7. At a meeting in Brazzaville in December, 1960, a group which became known as the Brazzaville Group or officially as The Union of African States and Madagascar, emerged. The Brazzaville Powers included Congo Brazzaville, Ivory Coast Senegal, Mauritania, Upper Volta, Niger, Dahomey, Chad. Gabon Central African Republic, Cameroon and

Madagascar. Since the invitation to this group was restricted, this was one of the first deliberate attempts to create a bloc of African states. In 1961 a second bloc was created at Casabalanca subsequently referred to as the Casablanca Group, the Casablanca Group comprising the more radical states at the time, namely Mali, Guinea, Ghana, Morocco and Alberia. In 1961 a conference of twenty states took place in the Liberian capital of Monrovia, including twelve states of the Brazzaville group as well as Liberia, Nigeria, Somalia, Sierra Leone, Togo, Ethiopia. Henceforward the lines of demarcation between the large moderate Monrovia bloc and the more radical Casablanca bloc shattered the political illusions of African unity. The development of an Organization of African Unity in 1963 was intended to re-cement African Unity.

8. Address to the National Assembly of the United Arab Republic, 9 April 1967 in Nyerere, Freedom and Socialism, Dar es Salaam, Oxford Univ. Press, 1968, pp. 294-5.

9. Press Conference text in Afrique Nouvelle, July 27, 1960.

10. For a discussion of the conflict between Nkrumah and Robert Gardiner on this point, see Michael L. Dei Anang, The Administration of Ghana's Foreign Relations 1957-65, London: Athelone Press, 1975, pp. 5-6.

11. See Robert Legvold, Soviet Policy in in West Africa, Cambridge: Harvard Univ. Press, 1970, for references and a general sense of Soviet Africa scholarship.

12. Philippe Schmitter, "A Revised Theory of Regional Integration," International Organization, Vol. XXIV, No. 4, 1970.

13. Ernst B. Haas, The Uniting of Europe; Political, Social and Economic Forces 1950-57, Stanford, Calif.: Stanford Univ. Press, 1958.

14. Ernst B. Haas, "Regional Integration; Reflection on the Joy and Anguish of Pretheorizing," International Organization, Vol. XXIV, No. 4, 1970.

15. Ernst B. Haas, Beyond the Nation-States: Functionalism and International Organization, Stanford, Calif.: Stanford Univ. Press, 1964.

16. Haas concentrated his own work outside of Europe on Central and Latin America, i.e., Ernst B. Haas and Philippe Schmitter, "Economics and Differential Patterns of Integration;

Projections about Unity in Latin America," International Organization, XVIII, Autumn, 1964.

17. Ernst B. Haas, "Joy and Anguish of Pretheorizing," op. cit., p. 610.

18. See for example Philippe Schmitter, "Further Notes on Operationalizing Some Variables Related to Regional Integration," International Organization, Vol. XXIII, Spring, 1969; and Philippe Schmitter, "A Revised Theory of Regional Integration," International Organization, Vol. XXIV, No. 4, Autumn, 1970.

19. See for example Abdul A. Jalloh, The Politics and Economics of Regional Political Integration in Central Africa (Unpublished Ph.D dissertation, University of California, Berkeley, 1969); Isebill V. Gruhn, Functionalism in Africa: Scientific and Technical Cooperation (Unpublished Ph.D thesis, University of California, Berkeley, 1967).

20. Karl W. Deutsch, et. al., Political Community and the North Atlantic Area, Princeton Univ. Press, 1957.

21. Green and Seidman, Unity or Poverty, op. cit.

'Marxist' is intended as a very loose designation to refer to both self identified Marxists as well as those who argue in favor of change in the international capitalistic structure.

22. See for example, Pierre Jalee, The Third World in World Economy, New York: Monthly Review Press, 1969; ________, The Pillage of the Third World, New York: Monthly Review Press, 1968.

23. Ibid., Jalee, Pillage, pp. 178-266.

24. See for example Donald S. Rothchild, ed., Politics of Integration, Nairobi: East African Publishing House, 1968; Joseph S. Nye, Jr., Pan-Africanism and East African Integration, Cambridge, Mass.: Harvard Univ. Press, 1965; Abdul A. Jalloh, Political Integration in French-Speaking Africa, Berkeley: Institute of International Studies, University of California, 1973.

25. Ernst B. Haas, The Obsolescence of Regional Integration Theory, Berkeley: Berkeley Institute of International Studies, University of California, 1975, p. 17.

26. Ibid., p. 14.

27. Ibid.

28. Ibid., p. 10.

29. Ibid., p. 9.

30. Ibid., p. 10.

31. This may be best illustrated by the Lome Convention; see Isebill V. Gruhn, "Inching Towards Interdependence: The Lomé Convention," International Organization, Vol. 30, No. 2, Spring 1976.

32. DECLARATION AND ACTION PROGRAMME ON THE ESTABLISHMENT OF A NEW INTERNATIONAL ECONOMIC ORDER, UN General Assembly Resolutions 3201 (S-VI) and 3202 (S-VI) May 1, 1974.

33. CHARTER OF ECONOMIC RIGHTS AND DUTIES OF STATES, UN General Assembly, Resolution 3281 (XXIX), December 12, 1974.

34. For an exxcellent discussion of the evolution of political and substantive matters, see Branislav Gosovic and John Gerard Ruggie, "On the creation of a new international economic order: issue linkage and the Seventh Special Session of the UN General Assembly," International Organization, Vol. 30, No. 2, Spring, 1976.

35. Ibid., Gosvic and Ruggie; see especially pp. 328-41 for a breakdown of the issues and positions of participants at the Seventh Special Session.

36. For a summary of the demands of the South, and the offers of the North, see Zdenek Cervenka, "Funeral in Paris," Africa, No. 71, July, 1977, pp. 55-57.

37. See for example, Jan Tinberg (co-ordinator), Reshaping the International Order: A Report to the Club of Rome. New York, E.P. Dutton and Co., 1976, and Mahbub ul Haq, The Poverty Curtain: Choices for the Third World, New York, Columbia Univ. Press, 1976.

38. See for example, Timothy M. Shaw, "The International Politics of Southern Africa: Change or Continuity," Issue, Vol. VII, No. 1, Spring, 1977, p. 24; Timothy M. Shaw, "The Political Economy of African International Relationship," Issue, Vol. V, No. 4, Winter, 1975.

# 3
# ECA's Organizational Structure, Leadership, Staff and Budget

## Leadership and Staff

Robert Gardiner, whose influence dominated the ECA for over a decade, can best be described as a national and international civil servant. He is a gentleman, a man of moderation at a time when moderation has not always been the order of the day, in Africa or anywhere else. Gardiner's aim throughout the 1960s was to make the ECA respectable in the eyes of African governments and of the international donor community. He was inclined to present himself to African heads of state as their servant, rather than as a lobbyist for a specific cause or organization; he did make it known that he favored regional cooperative arrangements for Africa, but he did so without flair.

Gardiner's style and posture left their mark on the ECA staff. All members of the staff were to understand that care should be taken not to offend member governments; documents and studies were to be written in a fashion that would urge action, or show the feasibility of a project, without in any way criticizing the past or present policies of any government. The ECA was to stay out of the fray that was African politics (although of course it frequently got into the fray, what with the Anglophone-Francophone schism and OAU-ECA antagonism).

In the international realm the ECA also sought to play a moderate and moderating role. The Commission presented itself as an arm of the UN's gentleman's club: bureaucratically reliable, trustworthy. By the mid'60s, a visit to Washington, D.C., from Robert Gardiner came as a positive relief to the US aid establishment, after the more flamboyant and radical style of Diallo Telli and the shrill tones of the OAU.[1] Gardiner came as a UN official, spoke in familiar tones, and, echoing the Western academic and policy-making wisdom of the time, favored regional integration for Africa. He pleaded, sensibly, for funding for background studies, technical assistance, and manpower training; he sharpened the aid establishment's understanding of African states' needs in these areas. Thus Gardiner's diplomatic style, while failing to make much of an impression on the African continent, gained him and the ECA international respectability in the 1960s.

Gardiner's administrative style at the ECA was low-keyed and erratic. Neither he nor the staff he attracted could be described as part of a highly-charged group of idea men; unlike Raul Prebisch at the ECLA, Gardiner was not interested in setting up a brain trust. Instead he sought to create a bureaucratic structure which paralleled the various sectorial divisions of the UN system, and which was charged with doing fairly mundane background work.

Gardiner himself worked with a small group of trusted staff members who, whenever the occasion arose, were asked to drop whatever study or project they were doing at the moment and undertake a new one. The consequences of having a sort of kitchen cabinet doing crash studies were twofold. First, an individual's knowledge or expertise was frequently less important than was his relationship with Gardiner when it came to being assigned to specific tasks; this practice had a negative effect on the staff as a whole. Second, the work of even the most select staff tended to be done at random, since there was no discernible intellectual framework within which to organize their activities. There was a small number of genuine technical experts, but they worked relatively autonomously--frequently as one-man operations. Generalists who were not part of Gardiner's inside group were under-utilized, and their work lacked direction; generalists who _were_ part of the inner circle were overworked (in the sense that they were given a vast number of tasks and never enough time to complete them) but they too lacked a sense of intellectual direction.

In 1968, about 60% of the professional staff of the ECA was African; by 1976 this figure was closer to 80%. Today the Divisions and Sections that make up the ECA's structure are, with a few exceptions, headed by Africans. Staffing problems have been something of a vicious circle for the ECA, since it replicates at the continental level the manpower shortage that exists at the national level; in this respect the African continent is in a uniquely adverse position, compared to other parts of the Third World. The ECA competes not only with national governments and private industry for trained manpower, but also with other international and inter-African organizations. When the ECA came into existence, the supply of University-trained Africans with development skills was so limited that the ECA, unlike the ECLA, was staffed largely by a heterogenous group of expatriates--UN public servants. Even as more Africans became available for international service, the ECA, given its low profile in Africa in general and its unpopularity in French-speaking countries in particular, commanded low priority. As the 1970s began, it was still reinforcing, rather than trying to reverse, its difficulties in Africanizing its staff and in attracting creative intellects.

It would be appropriate here to say a few words regarding the ECA's non-African staff. UN staff members assigned to the ECA, unlike those serving in the Specialized Agencies (where the international character of the staff is accepted), were aware from the beginning that their presence was stop-gap. Whatever their abilities and talents, expatriate ECA staff members assumed that their tenure there was going to be brief, and they consequently tended to be demoralized; Gardiner's habit of working with an African inner circle further lowered morale. The key exceptions to this rule were, again, those technical experts whose intellectual interests lay in applying their expertise to African circumstances; they worked on their special projects, as they had before in other UN agencies or in colonial services, and remained largely unconcerned about the policies and direction of the ECA as such.

Most of the Africans on the Staff were, from the very beginning, social scientists. Economists, lawyers and sociologists dominated; few natural scientists, engineers, or other scientific or technical expertise were included. The general complexion of the staff was that of generalists whose training prepared them for administrative work but whose background was unsuited for the technical aspects of development planning. For example, it would be more typical to find an agricultural economist or an industrial economist on the staff than an agronomist or steel industry expert. Similarly, lawyers and broadly trained sociologists were more likely to draft general policy statements and documents of organizational intentions than to develop and implement 'action programs' in public health, education or manpower training. In recent years there has been a slight change, but overall strengths and weaknesses continue to be essentially the same. In this respect the ECA resembles UN headquarters' administrative staff more than it resembles a technical division of one of the UN's Specialized Agencies.

A fairly large proportion of the African staff in the 1960s had come to the ECA early in its existence, preferring it to national service at a time when the political climate in their own countries seemed uncongenial. (Several Ghanaians, for example, including Gardiner, were attracted to the ECA during Kwame Nkrumah's regime.) This meant, of course, that they were unlikely to wield influence in the political ranks of the countries from which they had, in effect, defected. Unlike the ECLA, the ECA was less likely to be in a position to have its ideas brought to the attention of national ministries. A number of the African staff members at the ECA today have been there since the early '60s; they have become disassociated from the political life of their own countries and, more importantly, have lost contact with the economic and social life there. (Ironically, an exception to this pattern is Gardiner himself who, after he left the ECA , returned to Ghana and became, until his resignation in May, 1978, its Commissioner for Economic Planning.) More recent arrivals at the ECA may well effect changes in the years to come, but it is too early to know what their career patterns might be: will they move around within the UN system, go back to their home governments, or become career ECA staff members?

When Gardiner retired from the ECA in 1975, his leadership had managed to gain the ECA some international respectability, but had not convinced many people on the African continent that the organization was a potent regional instrument. The ECA's low profile obscured some of the real contributions that it had made (which will be discussed in the next chapter). Indeed, member governments were frequently so unfamiliar with the ECA's work that they were unable to make use of it.

Neither were Gardiner's leadership and style capable of producing an organizational ideology or sense of intellectual excitement that would inspire dedication in his staff. He made commendable progress in Africanization of the staff, but never overcame the demoralization associated with the Africanization process; and the efficiency of staff members was affected by uncertainty about the direction of the organization.

Yet with all these problems, it was not a purely public-relations comment on the part of Adedeji, the new executive secretary of the ECA, when he said, after a year with the organization, that the ECA "is an instrument of great potential in the hands of the member states. It is as useful as they wish to make it. There is no other regional organization in Africa today that has the accumulated experience and knowledge and the technical capabilities of the Commission to help in the economic integration and development of the continent."[2]

## Adebayo Adedeji

It is probably too early to assess the effect that the new executive secretary, Adebayo Adedeji, will have on the ECA. He was educated abroad--he has an MA in public administration from Harvard and a Ph.D in economics from the University of London--but returned to his own country, Nigeria, to serve as a Federal Commissioner, as Minister of Economic Development and Reconstruction, and as a university professor. His varied background would seem to be appropriate to the task of leading the ECA; his reputation would suggest that he is a man of a more political disposition than Gardiner--one whose approach to member governments might be less that of a servant than of a lobbyist or salesman. What is still unknown is whether Adedeji will, given the complexity of the UN employment structure, be able to replace some of the deadwood on his staff with dynamic new people, and whether under his guidance (or under that of the people he assigns leadership roles) the ECA can develop intellectual content, self-definition, and a strategy. The evidence available now is insufficient for coming to even preliminary conclusions on the matter.

One thing that is known, however, is that Adedeji has every reason to be familiar with the ECA's problems, both inside the organization and in the perceptions most Africans have of it. In 1970 he was one of a team of three experts asked to evaluate the policies and priorities of the ECA's manpower training program. The evaluation process involved reviewing the work of the ECA's secretariat, its conferences, seminars, documents--but it also involved country studies and team visits to seven African countries. If the team's fairly critical report is any indication, Adedeji will find it easy to see that the problems in the particular area he studied can also be found in other ECA activities.[3] The report commented on the lack of a focused program: the ECA, it said, did not have "a program in this field of manpower but merely a bunch of strung-together activities . . . Governments were ill-informed about ECA activities; there were too many disparate seminars and meetings, and little coordination and coherency." The reported noted again and again the absence of a plan and the lack of an overall objective.[4]

Adedeji was an active participant on the team that made this report; one would thus be justified in expecting him to have some sense of the ECA's internal and external problems. Whether his administrative talents and political capacities are equal to solving the problems he has identified is as yet an unanswered question. Early unease among staff members should not be taken as condemning evidence; indeed, the necessary house-cleaning would entail alienating those members of the staff who are too adjusted to their daily routines. Similarly, Adedeji's frequent absence from ECA headquarters can be interpreted either as interest in guaranteeing the survival of the ECA in the UN system or as lack of interest in developing a program he can sell to governments and organizations inside and outside Africa. In any event, the problems of staff and direction of the ECA demand Adedeji's early and serious attention.

## The ECA's Budget

In the most literal sense a budget is a document, containing words and figures, which proposes expenditures for certain items and purposes. The words describe items of expenditure or purposes, and the figures are attached to each item or purpose. Presumably, those who make a budget intend that there will be a direct connection between what is written in it and future events. Hence we might conceive of a budget as intended behavior, as prediction.

. . . The budget thus becomes a link between financial resources and human behavior to accomplish policy objectives. Only through observation, however, is it possible to determine the degree to which the predictions postulated in the budget turn out to be correct.[5]

The Economic Commission for Africa began its operations in 1958 with a budget of US $500 thousand; by 1968 its budget had grown to $4.65 million, and by 1976 to $9,108,474. A breakdown, by percentage, of the amounts allocated to the various divisions of the ECA might be useful for an understanding of the ECA's current areas of emphasis;[6]

| | |
|---|---|
| Agriculture | 8.5% |
| Development planning | 22.0 |
| Education and training | 3.3 |
| Human settlements | 2.3 |
| Industrial development | 10.4 |
| International trade | 6.3 |
| Labor management and employment | 1.7 |
| Natural resources | 8.8 |
| Population | 1.4 |
| Public administration | 1.9 |
| Public finance | 3.4 |
| Science and technology | 3.9 |
| Social development | 6.2 |
| Statistics | 13.8 |
| Transportation, communication and tourism | 6.6 |
| Total | 100.5%* |

*Does not add to 100% due to rounding error.

Breakdown By Program and Dollars for 1976-77*

| Program # | Total Allotment | Program |
|---|---|---|
| UN H-09-101 | $ 89,046 | Policy making organs |
| UN H-09-110 | 306,143 | Executive direction and management |
| UN H-09-210 | 419,137 | Agriculture and forest |
| UN H-09-240 | 974,947 | Dev planning production and policy |
| UN H-09-260 | 149,089 | Education and training |
| UN H-09-290 | 109,804 | Human settlements |
| UN H-09-330 | 472,778 | Industrial development |
| UN H-09-340 | 298,663 | International trade |
| UN H-09-440 | 78,678 | Labour management and employment |
| UN H-09-460 | 396,342 | Natural resources |
| UN H-09-480 | 63,378 | Population |
| UN H-09-500 | 83,226 | Public administration and finance |
| UN H-09-510 | 159,468 | Public finance |
| UN H-09-530 | 170-429 | Science and technology |
| UN H-09-530 | 279,360 | Social development |
| UN H-09-540 | 640,879 | Statistics |
| UN H-09-590 | 308,848 | Transport |
| UN H-09-710 | 987,654 | Conference services |
| UN H-09-790 | 354,812 | Management of technical cooperation |
| UN H-09-800 | 2,765,793 | Administration and common services |
| Total | $9,108,474 | |

A look at the ECA's current and future work programs shows that they call for heavy emphasis on the development of science and technology (especially in the realm of so-called 'appropriate technology') in industry, agriculture, and institution-building. The social development division calls for a variety of projects and programs requiring the development of appropriate technologies, technology centers, and information banks. But it is improbable that the staff and supporting resources affordable under the ECA's allocation of 3.9% of its budget to science and technology can cope with this work load. Any budget breakdown points not merely to priorities but to actual and

*All budgetary figures and analysis come from UN ECA Program Budget 1966-77 M75-317. See Appendix III for 1979-81 figures.

potential capacities--which ought to be borne in mind when existing work programs are evaluated and when future policy is being discussed. The ECA's actual capacity is obviously not quantifiable in the same way its budget breakdown is; a 22% allocation does not guarantee a 22% work capacity, nor does it guarantee the quality of the work. But it is difficult to imagine that a division that is allocated less than 4% of the organization's resources will have the manhour capacity (not to mention the staff quality and efficiency) to serve 20% of the organization's programs. The ECA budget, then, serves not only as a reflection of organizational policy priorities, but to some extent as a crude indicator of organizational capacity under optimal circumstances.

The same sort of inconsistency is evident in the fact that, of a continent that is predominantly agricultural, only 8-1/2% of the ECA's budget is allocated to agriculture. Such a small amount could be justified were there an official ECA policy to let the FAO handle the continent's agricultural needs. However, nothing in the ECA's work programs of the last 20 years would lead one to conclude that the ECA <u>has</u> followed such a policy. Therefore, the low budget allocation probably reflects a misplaced emphasis in the ECA's work program, and low institutional capacity in the agricultural development field.

While a look at the ECA's budgetary allocations is useful in an examination of the several issues involved in this study, considering the ECA as an autonomous body presents certain dangers that the reader should bear in mind. Since the ECA is part of the UN system, its budget stands in relation to the UN budget in much the same way a US state budget stands in relation to the federal budget. The way in which tasks are allocated among organizational mechanisms is partially responsible for budgetary emphasis. So a low budget for education, for example, may indicate either a lack of interest on the ECA's part in education, or an ECA/UNESCO decision that UNESCO will be the one to concern itself with African educational matters. Therefore, for a complete analysis of the ECA budget, the total UN system budget for Africa should probably be examined. However, even if we limit ourselves in the interests of focusing more closely on the ECA, it may still be possible to detect some trends and tendencies that will further our discussion.

The ECA budget is dependent on two major sources of income: its regular budget as part of the UN system, and additional resources made available to the ECA under bilateral[7] and multilateral programs. The main contributors to the latter are:[8]

- The United Nations Regional Program of Technical Assistance;
- The UNDP Inter-country (regional) Program of Technical Assistance;
- The UN Fund for Population Activities;
- Extra-budgetary resources provided through UN headquarters or through UN agencies; and
- Bilateral technical cooperation arrangements.

Let us look at the fiscal year 1975 as an example. In that year, the ECA received US $515,000 in convertible currencies under the regular UN Regional Program of Technical Assistance. From UN special measures for the least developed countries $408,500 was made available to the ECA; $38,400 was provided by UN headquarters for a seminar on statistical standardization in external transactions. UNDP funds amounting to $458,700 were sent to the ECA through UNCTAD, and the UN Fund for Population Activities alloted the ECA $337,560 for its own activities in that area. In addition an estimated total of $3,690,282 was sent to the ECA by various donor governments and organizations under bilateral technical cooperation arrangements; these funds made possible a total of 56 projects.[9] Thus, the ECA's regular budget from the UN is supplemented with external bilateral and multilateral funding, referred to by the ECA as "other extra budgetary."

The ECA owes a good deal to bilateral donations from industrial states. The overwhelming majority of these bilateral funds take the form of the financing of experts who either work in the ECA secretariat or serve in one of the ECA's programs in the field. In a few instances bilateral funding pays for an adviser who is assigned, under the auspices of the ECA, to work for a national government or institution. (Usually the donor countries provide the funds for one of their own nationals to be assigned to the ECA or an ECA-related activity but sometimes they will finance the recruitment and hiring of an expert in a certain field, regardless of national origin.) Thus bilateral contributions make it possible for the ECA to help African states finance and recruit necessary manpower--and help the ECA meet its own manpower needs as well.

Even with the help of these bilateral donations, it is still a tedious and time-consuming task to identify and recruit experts to augment the staff of the ECA secretariat or to help with project development and maintenance. But the importance of the roles played by these experts--whose fields of experience range from demography to dairy-farming, from forestry to correspondence education--is immeasurable. These short-term, donor-controlled funds and recruits have often made the difference between sustaining some sort of quality in the technical work of the ECA, and allowing it (in some fields) to be operational at all. Although the experts employed through these funds have not been of uniformly high quality, most of the high-quality technical work that has been done at the ECA or under ECA auspices would probably have not been done without these short-term specialists.

It is a sad but supportable comment on the UN--on its sluggishness, over-bureaucratization, shortage of funds, and quality of personnel--that the ECA has discovered that when it has an immediate need for a person of high technical competency and expertise, it is cheaper and more efficacious to recruit outside the UN system. In fact, many individuals within the ECA have found that a good relationship with a particular donor is absolutely essential to achieving any success with a program. This method of funding has its problem, of course. Given the relatively small total amount of bilateral financing available to the ECA and the relatively small number of experts it supports (30-50) one can see how small the ECA's scale of activity is--how for all their helpfulness, these experts are a drop in the bucket, considering Africa's needs. And yet some of the ECA's major contributions to African development have been made possible by this resource. A single regional advisor whose grasp of problems is good, whose advice is sound, and whose utilization around Africa is maximized, can make an impact incalculably greater than the cost of his salary.

When the ECA is given funds for the support of an expert that the ECA itself has designated, the employment of such an expert can help meet a programmatic need, although choosing one is often a tedious process. But this freedom of choice is not always available, since bilateral donors sometimes stipulate areas of interest for reasons of their own--and if the ECA wants their funding, their plans must be integrated or appended to the ECA's program. The difficulties involved in this manner of staffing and program development are obvious.

I have just argued that without bilateral funding, both the staff and operations of the ECA would look genuinely hopeless. But I would like to suggest also that there are serious disadvantages for the ECA in having become so donor-dependent. Bilateral donors usually have their demands, although these vary from country to country. Aid from the United States, West Germany and Japan is usually tied, both in terms of personnel and project; for example, a country will offer the funds and staffing for road X and not road Y. The ECA and the recipient government may have decided that from the point of view of national or regional development, road Y would be more useful; but an independent investigation would reveal that the donor country's desire to build road X has a precise reason--such as providing an easier way to move exports that are of interest to the donor country. So neither the ECA nor the recipient country has much choice in the matter--but both would prefer to have the help for road X than none at all, so road X is built.

Other bilateral donors, especially the Scandinavian countries, do not tie their aid to an individual expert or project, but may tie it to an area of ideological preference, such as women, youth, or rural development. Over the long run this may cause the ECA's work program to reflect the availability of bilateral resources, or current international donor fashions, rather than client needs. When it was fashionable to think of all development as industrial, donors were willing to finance industrial development experts. Today, when appropriate technology, or the role of women in development has caught the fancy of international development thinking, the ECA may find that most of its bilateral funding will come earmarked for these sectors. One can argue of course, that since Africa's need for expertise in development areas is so vast, the ECA would be well-advised to use whatever bilateral funding is made available to it. But is it well-advised to depend heavily on external determination of the priorities of its budget?

One can also argue that all the influence of bilateral funding means is that the ECA's budget does not reflect client or organizational priorities *alone*. Robert Gardiner's efforts to seek bilateral funding should be seen in the context of a shortage of international capital resources to carry out the ECA's work; similarly, the current emphasis on the funding of technical expertise should be understood in the context of the African continent's and the ECA's own lack of such expertise. However, the fact that the tail has frequently been allowed to wag the dog when it comes to budgetary allocations has presented the ECA with two dilemmas. One is that the ECA's fuzzy image, as well as its hat-in-hand approach to potential donors, may have encouraged donors to assert their preferences rather than allow the ECA to use its own discretion in budgetary planning. The other dilemma is that the shortage of expertise on the ECA s own staff, along with the vast manpower needs of its clients, have produced in the ECA a bilateral-donor-dependency--in the formulation and execution of its work program as well as in the determination of its budget.

Hence, the ECA's budget must ultimately be seen as a complex mixture of the objectives of the organization and those of the bilateral donors. Those among the ECA's clientele who, whether beneficiaries of bilateral funding or not, accuse the ECA of allowing itself to be dominated by forces outside Africa, are probably less enthused than others about the fact that Robert Gardiner increased the ECA's capital and manpower resources by augmenting its regular UN budget with bilateral aid.

## The ECA's Organizational Structure

Studying an organizational structure, especially in a relatively small and somewhat personalized organization, tends to both clarify and confuse one's understanding of the nature of the organization. Organizational structure may tell one less than one might like about the actual quality of the organization's work, or about its effectiveness to clients. On the other hand, studying the structure may reveal some information on the limits, bottlenecks, oversights, inefficiencies, and emphases of an organization.

The ECA's past forms of organizational structure and its present plans for reorganization have had to be rationalized to suit the wider UN family, as well as the ECA and its African clients. Hence discussions of the ECA headquarters' organization and reorganization, and of the development of ECA-sponsored subregional institutions, are one of the best sources of information when one is analyzing ECA thinking regarding inter-African cooperation and integration over the years. These discussions are also a good source of information on internal ECA struggles to develop an organizational ideology that can address an ever-changing African and international environment.

At this point in the discussions, the ECA has a range of alternatives. It could devote itself to administering all UN development projects in Africa; for instance, it could have its Industrial Development division work in collaboration with UNIDO and act as the latter's administrative arm in Africa. Or it could confine itself to research, feasibility studies, project development, and the staffing and funding of inter-African industrial development projects: all such projects involving more than one African country, either in their planning or in their execution, would be dealt with by the ECA. Or it could concern itself with inter-sectorial development, regardless of whether it is a project of concern to one African state or to several. In this last case, the ECA would not duplicate the work of UNIDO or the FAO, but rather would serve to coordinate the activities of the specialized agencies.

Neither the ECA's enunciated policies nor its organizational structure give any clue as to which of these alternatives it will choose for its future role. (Neither do any of them describe its past institutional capacity, for that matter.) The ECA has always claimed that inter-African development projects were its special terrain, and a good number of ECA feasibility studies propose multi-national or subregional arrangements. However, the ECA's work program has not confined itself to this terrain. The ECA has also, at various times, claimed that it ought to be the administrative arm for all UN projects in Africa; its organizational structure, modelled on the sectorial UN structure, certainly suggests this intention. Yet the ECA's skeletal staff in each section makes this alternative impossible without vastly increasing the ECA's work capacity. Even if the ECA chooses the less-improbable alternative of becoming the coordinator for inter-sectorial programs for African states, it would involve changes in the ECA's division-and-unit structure, if not restructuring the entire UN system.

ECA's organizational structure, to date, reflects an interplay and overlap and at times a contradiction resulting from the pursuit of different patterns of operation. A diversity of organizational and operational goals is built into the organizational structure and is further complicated by tensions and demands placed upon ECA's structure and operation due to the nature of its budget. How these contradictions and complexities have worked themselves out in practice can be illustrated by taking a closer look at the work of one of ECA's substantive divisions. ECA's industrial development division can serve as a particularly good example of how several organizational goals and budgetary complexity interact. Industrial development has been one of the early areas of emphasis for African development, and this emphasis was reflected in the organizational and budgetary attention given to the subject within the United Nations as a whole, within the ECA, and by African states themselves.

## Case Study: The ECA's Industrial Development Division

We will recall that in the 1950s and '60s, many people held excessively high expectations of rapid industrial development in Africa, in spite of the fact that agriculture accounted for 80% or more of each African country's economic activities. 1975 figures indicate that the 30% of the world's population that lives in developed countries produces 93% of the world's industrial output. This means that the share of world industrial production held by developing countries is only 7%, while their share of the population is 70%. Of this 7%, the African share is a miniscule 0.6%; its goal for the year 2000 is to raise that to 2%, more than tripling its output--a task which in itself is quite considerable.[10] So African industrial development is of little statistical importance on a global scale, and will probably continue to account for a very small part of African economic activity. But aside from the earlier (and frequently exaggerated) emphasis on African industrial development, industrial development planning is central to increased African self-reliance and to the realization of a New Economic Order.

It has been estimated that if the poor nations had been able to exercise the same amount of control over the processing and distribution of their exports as the rich nations do, and if they could receive for those exports the same proportion of the final consumer prices for them, the poor nations' export earnings might increase fivefold.[11] For African states, this would involve the development of industrial plants for processing agricultural goods, as well as the development of import substitution industries. Given the particularities of Africa, industrial development planning must also include attention to scale and markets, and therefore involves regional and subregional planning. In addition, the question of industrial development adds to the range of manpower and technology access and transfer issues that are central to many of the discussions related to the NIEO.

We will also recall that one of the false assumptions of early post-independence development thinking was related to the development of an LDC's industrial capacity. The ECA's early concentration on industrial development reflected international and African priorities of the 1950s and '60s; its budgetary allocations for industrial development work regularly equaled or exceeded its allocations for agricultural work, in spite of the fact that agriculture is the major economic activity of most African states. In addition, the ECA thought that its emphasis on inter-state cooperation was particularly applicable to feasibility studies and project formation in industry; it was often easier to argue that a West African steel industry required cooperation than to suggest that inter-state cooperation could raise agricultural productivity. Thus, the activities of the ECA tended to reflect the widely-held assumption that 'development' meant _industrial_ development, and in fact the ECA based its preference for regional cooperation and integration on this assumption.

A report issued after the Third Conference on African Ministers of Industry (held in 1976 in

Nairobi and sponsored jointly by the ECA and the OAU) reflected a new theoretical grasp of the role of industry in Africa.[12] The call for modernization through industrialization is not as frequently made as it was in ECA documents of the 1960s; the ministers take note of the external forces which, due to increased oil prices and international inflation, devastated African economies. The ministers have set a new goal for greater industrial self-reliance within the context of "rural industrialization, adaptation of technology, and the development and selection of appropriate technology" as well as that of the "interrelationship between technology and other sectors."[13] The report focuses on the link between industry and agriculture, and recognizes the importance of industries related to food production.

Several other factors indicate that Africans are facing contemporary realities and have learned lessons from past errors in their development planning. The ministers' report makes it plain that industry and agriculture must be seen in close developmental relationship to each other--in fact, that industrial development planning must be seen in 'package' terms. The development of an appropriate industry requires simultaneous environmental impact studies, manpower development, and national or multinational institution-building. The ministers also appear to sense that political will at both the national and inter-African levels is essential to the sort of coordination among sectors of society and across national boundaries that allows for economic progress.

The ministers at the meeting further recognized the fact that while there seemed to be a glut of institutions on the African continent, still, the development of certain institutions was important for progress;[14] these included an African Center for Consulting, Engineering and Management Services, and a regional Center for Design, Adaptation and Transfer of Technology.[15] The development of these centers is clearly in line with the ECA's policy of encouraging regional institutions; however, it also provides another opportunity for UN agencies to overlap and compete. At the industrial ministers' meeting, the executive director of UNEP stressed the environmental-impact aspects of the subjects under discussion. UNCTAD expressed concern over the trade aspects of technology transfers, and went over its past and planned activities in this field, while UNIDO called for the establishment of a new section devoted exclusively to the transfer of technology. ILO is interested in several aspects of these problems, and UNESCO is interested in information exchanges and training in the field of technology. FAO, while not mentioned specifically in the ministers' report, is engaged in the food industry and technology.

We can see that this 1976 meeting on industrial development in Africa compares favorably with earlier efforts: problems are seen more comprehensively, past failures are taken into account, and inter-governmental planning is more highly valued. However, increased sophistication in the perception of problems and possible solutions has not resulted in more coordination at the ECA or between the ECA and other UN agencies. The UN's so-called African-institution-building effort, as far as industrial development goes, is still on the drawing boards. Just as with research and training centers in other areas, the ECA (with the help of OAU co-sponsorship) has sought, and sometimes obtained, the support of African governments for these centers, but they are still less African inter-state institutions than they are extensions of the ECA and the UN.

Some of the ECA's real crises and failures can be understood within the context of this discussion of industrial development. The ECA's industrial development division commands 10.4% of its 1976 budget--only Development Planning and Statistics receive more. Thus the old misplaced emphasis on industry instead of agriculture still exists to a certain extent. Since this emphasis has persisted over a period of 20 years, one might assume that the ECA's industrial division would have acquired a special capacity for expertise, and that it might even have developed a sense of direction within the ECA and with regards to the other UN agencies. It therefore comes as a disappointment when one discovers that the industrial division is no better organized than it was ten years ago, and that this illustrates the rule rather than an isolated example of inefficiency afflicting the ECA.

In the spring of 1976 the staff of the industrial division was made up of 19 professionals, only four of whom were part of the ECA's permanent staff; of the rest, five were UNIDO-funded employees, five were FAO-supported, and five were paid out of bilateral funds. Twelve of the 19 are economists--a large proportion--but what is perhaps the strongest single group of experts is the five forestry specialists. There are also three agri-industry experts and two housing specialists on the division's staff.[16]

Like that of other ECA divisions, this staff does not work, by and large, in response to government requests; rather, it develops its own projects and programs and then tries to sell them to various governments. The fields of expertise represented in the division often determine the direction of its work. The quantity and expertise of the forestry staff have led to high-quality work in this field; but while there is no doubt that environmentally sound handling of forests and their related industrial development are important subjects, the current recognition accorded the ECA in this field is less the consequence of its own policy than of an accident of staff.

The realization that African industrial development must be seen as a package (integrating technology, management, salesmanship, etc.) has been reached by the ministers in their report, but the industrial division, as we can see in a numerical breakdown of its staff, does not have the capacity to provide 'package' services, except in isolated instances. This, along with some competition from the FAO and UNIDO, left the ECA with little idea of what its special role in industrial development should be. On those occasions when duplication of efforts was avoided, it was on a project-by-project, person-to-person basis (i.e., communication between an FAO-supported staff member and someone in his field at FAO), and not a consequence of a division of functions among agencies.

The industrial division is also afflicted with chronic permutations of its staff. It is generally recognized that it takes three or four years to develop and supervise a project or program. Yet almost one-quarter of the industrial division's staff serves bilaterally-funded, hence two-year, terms. This makes coordination of efforts and development of a policy direction impossible.

Another way of gauging ECA capacity in a specific field is to compare the current staff capacity to the requirements of projected programs. The Revised Medium-term Plan for 1976-81, for example, is symptomatic of the ECA's inability to live up to its own expectations.[17]

The Plan's stated aims for industrial development projects are "to harmonize African industrial policies and programs so as to facilitate the establishment of basic multinational industries; to promote the development of large-scale manufacturing for export based on African raw materials and other inputs; and to facilitate regional and international consultations to safeguard and promote collective interests in African countries."[18] This general statement, which is prefatory to the specifics of the work program, is noteworthy in that it stresses inter-African activities. As we will see, however, this emphasis is not stressed as strongly in the actual work program. The first set of projects in the program are concerned with lauching studies, collecting information, holding meetings and seminars, and sharing information and training. The proposed program does not guarantee that the uneven quality of the ECA's work up to now will be improved, or that the ECA will clarify its role (as opposed to those of the other UN agencies), or that a new set of ideas will guide these activities.[19]

The planned industrial development activities that fall under inter-state institution-building are also somewhat disjointed New studies, seminars, and workshops are planned; in fact, this section of the work program has the appearance of a grab bag--it's full of activities that are listed merely because they have been planned to take place somewhere within the larger UN structure. Such grab-bag activities include the meeting of machine-tool experts, held in cooperation with UNIDO, and the conference on the code of conduct for transnational cooperation, held under the auspices of the ECA and the UN Center on Transnational Cooperation. One should recall, however, that some of Africa's most successful inter-state organizations came out of just such meetings. The ECA's ongoing program for industrial development will continue to try to bring African governments together in the interests of developing inter-state mechanisms that will facilitate industrial development.

The industrial division's program for developing continental organizational extensions of the ECA lists a number of studies to be undertaken by the ECA in conjunction with UNIDO, regarding the establishment of various regional centers. It remains unclear, however, what the ECA's role is to be in the establishment of such centers, or what the precise relationship is between the centers and the ECA as an institution. The ECA apparently believes that there will be some institutional connection between it and the centers, and that no matter what form African governments' participation takes (i.e., direct participation, or participation through OAU cosponsorship), the centers will somehow remain tied to the UN structure of regional and specialized agencies.

The final section of the ECA's proposed work program in industrial development calls for fostering "the development of rural and small-scale industries as a means of stimulating employment in non-agricultural activities."[20] On first inspection it seems that these activities are intended to contribute to the international development assistance community to improve African national and regional capacities--but on closer examination it seems possible to include some of these activities as contributing to the development of African subregional and/or regional institution building. That is, some of the ECA's continuing and proposed activities in rural and small-scale industry will be taken up by existing or yet-to-be-developed African regional or subregional institutions, while others will be assumed by ECA-sponsored research and training institutions or subregional bureaus of the ECA secretariat. Problems will undoubtedly arise from the potential overlap of activities. As before, few references have been made to work of a similar nature that is being done by the FAO and UNIDO. Little indication is given in the work program as to what tasks involving small-scale and rural industry are to be carried out by the industrial development division, and which ones are to be left, for example, to the integrated rural development program of the social development division.[21]

The industrial division's work program is exemplary of ECA's structure, operations and diffuse goals. Activities lack a clear focus, and will probably suffer from a lack of coordination with other ECA activities or with the activities of other UN agencies. Priorities may have changed, but they are still not informed by an organizational ideology that distinguishes the ECA from other economic development agencies of the UN.

In addition, there is nothing in the proposed work program that would still the criticism that the ECA's many meetings and studies never seem to be part of a genuine program. Thus, neither the ECA nor the UN has developed a focus for its activities in the industrial development field.

Even if one supposes that this jumble of activities (many of which are, after all, useful, even necessary) constitutes an important contribution to African development, a second question comes up: does the industrial division of the ECA have the capacity to carry out the proposed work program? On the basis of my observation of the division in 1976, I would say that the projected program could not be carried out by the division's current staff. The program is probably based on the suggestions of the division itself, but it contains no critical examination of the capacity of the present staff and no guarantees regarding changes in and additions to that staff. This dilemma is evident throughout the work program. It is only a slight exaggeration to say of the ECA work program that the tail is frequently wagging the dog. That is, programs have been drawn up on the basis of various identified African needs, but without any reference to how and by whom they will be carried out--all that is left for later consideration.

As the matter now stands, several high-caliber experts in the industrial division will probably continue to produce useful individual work for which the ECA will probably receive credit. High-quality studies, reports, and consultancy services will continue to reflect the quality and conscientiousness of one expert rather than a comprehensive work program specifically designed for the ECA's industrial development division.

The industrial development division has to some extent in the past (and could in the future) played an important role in offering consultancy services to member states, with the idea of making them less dependent on bilateral aid, on the services rendered by multinational corporations with investment interests, or on industrial development experts paid on an _ad hoc_ basis out of national budgets. Industrial development is an area where trained African manpower is in short supply; even the ECA's industrial development division counts few Africans among its staff. Thus, African governments are dependent on consultants who in many cases are not particularly familiar with African circumstances, or are specialists who fail to take into account the industrial development 'package' needs of the LDCs. A Czech consultant asked to help with the establishment of a shoe industry may fail to take into account related needs in marketing and manpower training. Similarly, the industrial consultancy services made available through foreign corporations may not maximize an African country's interests, and, again, will probably not take into account African needs in areas related to the establishment of a particular industrial enterprise.

These examples suggest that in the industrial development field Africans need a vast amount of consultancy services that are oriented toward specifically African needs, and they need these at a lower price than they are paying now. It is difficult to think of an area where additional resources, made available through the NIEO in the interests of collective African self-reliance, are more urgently needed. The ECA's minimal headquarters staff is clearly insufficient to the task, even though its increased sophistication in relating industry to other aspects of development seems promising. The establishment of regional training institutions is a necessary step towards increasing continental capacity in the field of industrial development. The most promising step, however, probably lies in the direction of the development of subregional branches of ECA Headquarters. If high-quality industrial development experts are stationed in a subregion and work in conjunction with the subregion's governments, the ECA may yet play a role in meeting Africa's industrial needs. Mobile ECA consultants could replace bilaterally- or corporation-funded experts: not only would African states be able to cut their expenditures, but the quality of the consultant work would probably be improved and the ability to coordinate industrial development with development in other fields would probably be increased. In short, the ECA might come to play the middleman role, between international resources and local needs, for which a regional commission is ideally suited. However, the discrepancy between the ECA's skeletal headquarters staff and member-states' vast needs in the industrial development field demand that the ECA's role be further clarified;

it might have to reduce its range of activities in favor of higher-quality services in limited areas.

Recent Developments

So far I have shown that throughout its existence, ECA's organizational structure, its staff and its budget at the secretariat level have suffered from lack of a clear mission. In addition, its staff, measured quantitatively and qualitatively, has proven incapable of contending with a range of demands and has lacked resources to meet these demands. Staffing and budgetary restraints within the large international system of which ECA is a part, and within ECA itself, have also contributed to the fact that its activities are diffuse. ECA's leadership has sought to address some of these problems at various junctures during ECA's history. The most recent effort includes a proposal to reorganize the structure of ECA's secretariat. It can be noted, however, that the proposed structure constitutes a refinement of the existing sectorial structure. The new organizational structure does not promise a reduction in the number of roles and purposes which ECA has consistently sought to play and which have been critically commented upon in previous pages. According to available reorganization documents, the ECA is to be "put into a position to become the regional operating arm for sectors represented by the UN specialized agencies, such as FAO, and UNIDO."[22] This description does not say whether the ECA will, within that charge, wish to confine itself to inter-state or multi-sectorial matters, or whether it will seek to become the regional operating arm for <u>all</u> activities. The reorganization plan calls for some structural streamlining and some staff expansion, but nothing of the magnitude that would give the ECA the organizational capacity to "become the regional operating arm for the UN family of specialized agencies"--at least not in the foreseeable future. The ECA's latest policy statements and documents do not, it seems to me, suggest a more limited function for the organization than it has had before.

At the same time that the ECA is undertaking this reorganization, the UN system as a whole has been addressing the question of restructuring its Economic and Social sectors. The General Assembly established an *ad hoc* committee to study

## Revised Structure

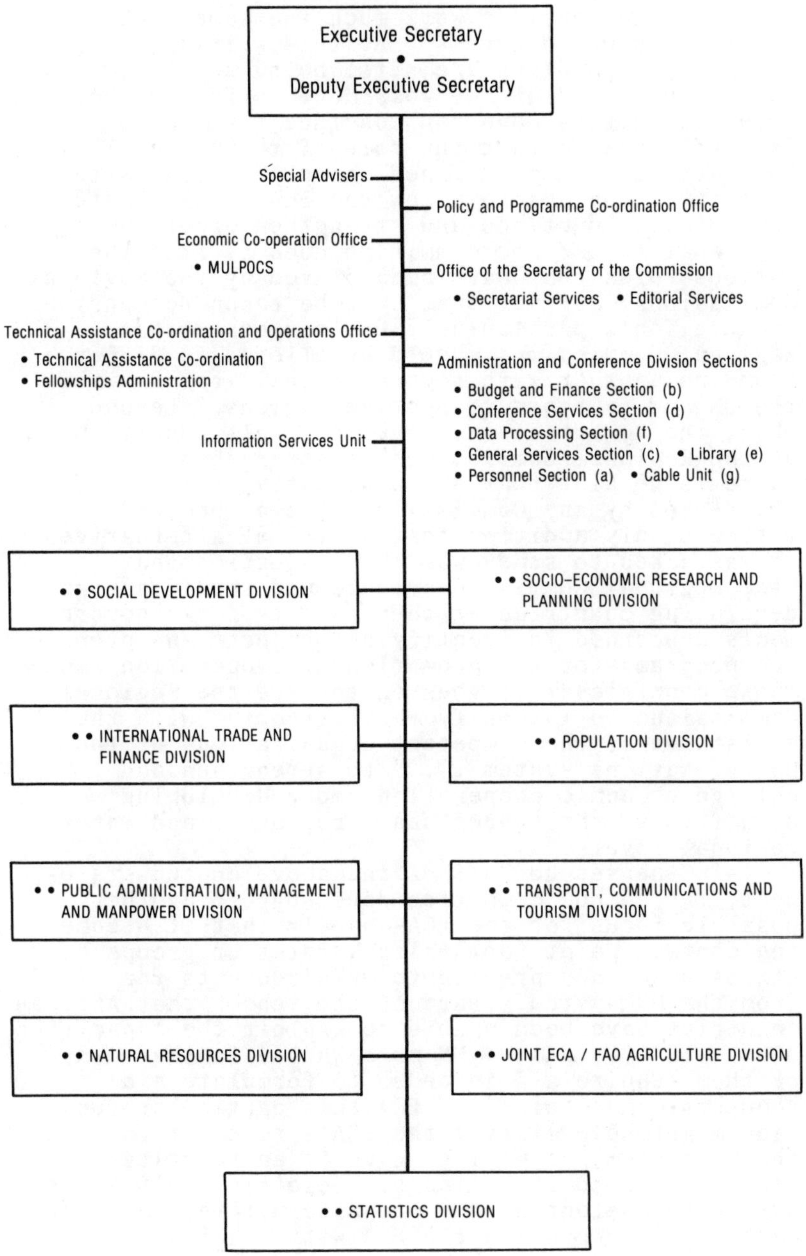

the matter, one of its duties was to look at the range of roles that the Regional Commission might be asked to play. The alternatives the Committee was asked to consider were much the same ones we have discussed here.[23] At this writing, UN reorganization plans are still being studied; but on the basis of the work done so far by the *ad hoc* committee, one can conclude that there *is little* chance that the role of the Regional Commissions will be defined sharply enough (with respect to the UN) to allow the ECA to eliminate some of its functions and strengthen others.

What the *ad hoc* committee does is list the various roles *that have* been played by the Regional Commissions, suggest that care be taken to consider each region's particularities, and state that Regional Commissions should be allowed to differ from one another with regard to their roles within the UN and in their respective regions. Beyond this, the committee only asks that all functions of the Regional Commissions be strengthened; there is no hint that any alternative role could be created by any Commission. The *ad hoc* committee's only addition to the list *of alternatives* it was asked to study was the suggestion that "the Regional Commissions concerned should assist developing countries at the request of the governments concerned in identifying projects and preparing programs for the promotion of cooperation among those countries"; it goes on to urge the Regional Commissions to intensify their efforts "with the assistance of the competent organizations of the United Nations system . . . to strengthen and enlarge economic cooperation among developing countries at the subregional, regional, and interregional levels."[24]

In the second half of the above-quoted statement, the *ad hoc* committee does suggest another possible *focus for* the ECA--namely that it become the contact point for African states or groups of states when they prepare to make requests for aid from the UN system. Part of the reason that African countries have been unable to exploit the capacities of the ECA (or of the UN as a whole) is that many of them require aid in order to formulate aid requests. Assigning the ECA this particular function might help clarify the ECA's role within the UN system, as well as give it an identity recognizable to its clients. Selecting this alternative (or selecting any *one* alternative, for that matter) would provide the *ECA* with a guide to restructuring its secretariat. However, by suggesting that the ECA share this new role with the specialized agencies--without suggesting clear lines of responsibilities for each--the *ad hoc* committee goes no further than UN reorganization rhetoric of the past in reducing inter-agency competition; it certainly doesn't help the ECA in its quest to find a clearly-defined role.

The *ad hoc* committee winds up its section on regional and inter-regional cooperation by cavalierly suggesting that "greater authority should be delegated to the Regional Commissions," but it fails to explain how this greater authority can be exercised without encroaching on the authority of the other segments of the UN system. Finally, the committee advises the Regional Commissions to "rationalize their structure, *inter alia*, by streamlining their subsidiary machinery."[25] It is difficult to see how streamlining an organizational structure can be expected to yield any success unless the functions of the Regional Commissions in general (and in the context of our discussion, the functions of the ECA in particular) are brought into some kind of focus. Neither ECA attempts at reorganizing itself nor UN attempts to fix the position of the Regional Commissions within the UN system have succeeded in delineating the tasks the ECA could best undertake. The ECA's budgetary and structural reforms must take place within the context of the entire UN system, which, rather than offend any one segment by making choices among them, tends to foster duplication of efforts and duties. In the absence of UN- or self-initiated ECA restructuring, the ECA's clients have every reason to continue to feel uncertain as to how they can have their interests represented in the UN maze.

If neither the UN's nor the ECA's plans for restructuring offer much hope that the role of the ECA within the UN system will become any better defined, hope *is* held out by one feature of the ECA's proposal for structural revision: the strengthening of the office of the executive secretary.[26] Under this part of the plan, the executive secretary would be responsible for coordinating the ECA and for fostering inter-African cooperation. While bureaucratic restructuring is no guarantee that a new direction will be taken, the new machinery could have the long-range effect of allowing for considerable change within the ECA.

At a time of financial stringency within the UN system however, it is unlikely that the ECA will be able to find the funds it will need to hire the senior officials asked for in the proposal. Under these circumstances, a reshuffling of the existing staff may be necessary; the staff at the division level could be reduced and that at the policy and planning level increased. This would force the ECA to limit itself to developing inter-African programs and institutions, and to get out of the business of competing with the specialized agencies in substantive areas. But even with this reshuffling, the ECA would have to hire a few new staff members and dispense with a few old ones, and under current UN personnel regulations the ECA is not in a position to do so. Reshuffling is therefore a problem of far greater magnitude than changing a few boxes on the organizational chart might suggest.

For an intellectual focus and a more narrowly-defined organizational role, we may have to look to those working directly under the executive secretary. While the structural change that gives them more authority was not proposed with the intention of weakening the sectors--in fact, the reports recommends that the sectorial divisions be strengthened[27]--it is unlikely that the large numbers of new people the sectorial divisions would require will be added to the ECA staff in the near future; the proposed restructuring may have the unintended consequence of making it possible for those at the top to hand down a more specific set of instructions as to the direction of sectorial activities.

Discussions of ECA restructuring also indicate that flexible task forces may be used to pool expertise from sectorial divisions for a specific tas: for example, rural development experts from the Social Development section and from the Agricultural division could be asked to work together on a specific study or project. This flexible use of existing staff may minimize the interference of the sectorial structure on proper work, and, in theory, could have desirable consequences--<u>if</u> a focus and direction informs these activities. One must remember that Robert Gardiner's use of some staff members for special assignments led to staff disorientation and demoralization. Making the ECA's structure more flexible may result in better use of staff, but will only do so within the context of a comprehensive organizational ideology.

## Sub-Regional Structure

This discussion of the ECA's structure has so far been confined to the secretariat at its headquarters. I would like to turn now to the ECA's subregional offices, which were created at the ECA's Fourth Session in 1962 "with a view to decentralizing the Commission's activities" and to "improving the efficiency of the Commission." Four subregional offices were established: for West Africa in Naimey, for North Africa in Tangiers, for East Africa in Lusaka, and for Central Africa in Kinshasa.[28] At the time of the Fourth Session, the idea of developing subregional institutions was very much a part of contemporary thinking about African development. In fact, direct and indirect comments in documents from that time suggested that these subregional offices should become the nuclei for African regional cooperation and integration.

However, for reasons that are by now obvious, these offices never succeeded in decentralizing the ECA, nor in aiding subregional development; the ECA's manpower and financial shortages were multiplied in the field. While certain individuals in the subregional offices did at times give good, if localized, advice, or help get a project off the ground, it was not possible for the ECA to have a strong outreach program. In addition, neither the political nor economic time was right for subregional activities; as we know, the slow disintegration in the 1960s of such regional arrangements as the East African Common Market did not lead governments to search for new bases for regional integration. As a consequence, the ECA's subregional offices stagnated.

By the 1970s, UN headquarters had taken the initiative in addressing the problem of developing advisory services that would be responsive to sub-groups of states. The General Assembly created the United Nations International Multidisciplinary Development Advisory Teams (UNDATs). Of the seven UNDATs established at the time, three were located in Africa; one at Yaounde in the United Republic of Cameroon, one at Naimey in Niger, and one at Lusaka in Zambia. The work of these UNDATs will be discussed in the following chapter; suffice it to say here that the teams were, structurally speaking, instruments of UN headquarters, although they were supposed to work in conjunction with the

ECA. The UNDATs were originally funded bilaterally for the most part, but no long-term financing was ever arranged; when the bilateral funds dried up in 1975, the Africa-based teams were financed on a temporary basis by the UNDP while a joint ECA/UNDP evaluation group studied the teams' future.[29]

With the establishment and development of the UNDATs, the ECA's largely inoperative subregional offices gradually went out of business, becoming absorbed by the UNDATs. Subsequently, the ECA in its evaluation of the role of the UNDATs was forced to consider whether or not it wanted some kind of subregional mechanism at all. The ECA's dream of developing the nuclei for regional integration had vanished by 1976, but the desire to have a subregional structure persisted.

Executive Secretary Adedeji stated in a 1977 interview that "in order to foster economic cooperation at subregional levels and to facilitate the implementation of these projects, we are converting our existing subregional offices into Multinational Programming and Operational Centers (MULPOCs). They will be operational arms of the Commission at the subregional level."[30] Technically speaking, these MULPOCs will replace both the UNDATs and the ECA subregional offices. In addition, three new centers are being planned: one for Central Africa (Burundi, Rwanda and Zaire), one for North Africa (Algeria, Egypt, Libyan Arab Republic, Morocco, and the Sudan), and one for the coastal countries of West Africa (Benin, Ghana, Guinea-Bissau, the Ivory Coast, Liberia, Nigeria, Sierra Leone, and Togo). This leaves the former Naimey UNDAT to serve the Sahel countries of West Africa (Gambia, Mali, Mauritania, the Niger, Senegal, and Upper Volta). What is perhaps more important for the ECA is that the MULPOCs are meant to have a new kind of structural relationship to ECA headquarters: MULPOC work programs are to be integrated into the ECA work program (the way those of the old subregional offices were supposed to be), and, unlike the UNDATs, the MULPOCs are to be the true operational arms of the ECA.[31] Looking at the ECA's revised organization chart, we can see that the old subregional offices and the UNDATs fell under the jurisdiction of the ECA's Economic Cooperation office--which in turn was under the direct supervision of the executive secretary. Therefore the supervision of the MULPOCs can be expected to fall to the executive secretary's office as well.

The discussion in the following chapter of the program of work of the MULPOCs will show their significance; I will only say here that with the establishment of the MULPOCs (and the conversion of the old UNDATs into MULPOCs), the ECA will continue to have a subregional structure. Desirable as this is from a structural point of view, however, it is no guarantee that the dysfunctional aspects we have seen in the organization of the ECA's headquarters will not be repeated at the MULPOC's level. But if the MULPOCs can help deliver international development resources to African states--individually or collectively--this structural change will bring the ECA closer to its clients than it is now in its somewhat removed bureaucratic fortress in Addis Ababa.

Given the present divisions within the international community (made manifest at international conferences held under UN auspices in the past few years), it seems unlikely that radical restructuring of the UN system will happen in the near future. It seems equally unlikely that new sources of funds will spring up soon. Under these circumstances, becoming the regional operational arm of the UN is an unrealistic goal for the ECA.

A more realistic goal might be to generate the capacity and creativity needed to build inter-African programs, projects, and institutions. To achieve this the ECA should develop a high-quality think-tank; it should make the kind of staff readjustments that show an emphasis on organizational ideology, on intellectual direction, on high-powered studies of African regional and subregional development. Once the ECA decides on such an emphasis, no more energy will be wasted on the debate, long carried out in ECA documents and in conversations with ECA officials, over which activity--pilot programs, studies, or action programs--the ECA should engage in. Instead the ECA could concentrate on the one belief it has held, however weakly, throughout its history: that inter-state cooperation, coordination, and integration are essential to African development. An organization that devotes itself to serving this need with sensible programs, projects, and institutions could well make a mark on African affairs. The proposed restructuring of the ECA does not preclude a move in such a direction, as I have said but it does not guarantee such a move, either. One must therefore remain uncertain as to whether a clear and realistic direction for the organization has yet been found.

## Conclusion

The United Nations Economic Commission for Africa has, since its inception in 1958, received more than its share of adverse publicity. All organizations concerned with the monumental problems of the LDCs have come under fire at some time, both from the disenchanted industrial world and the disheartened Third and Fourth Worlds, but the ECA has received unusually harsh criticism. It has been denounced as the archetypical UN agency: overly bureaucratic, constantly in competition with itself, always duplicating or failing to coordinate its work, endlessly producing meaningless and largely unread studies, and carelessly arranging its budget so that 60% or more goes to administrative costs rather than 'action programs.'

Criticism is also aimed at the ECA itself. The ECA, unlike the ECLA, has always lacked an intellectual focus; there may be disagreement over the outlook and program that Raul Prebisch advocated during his leadership of the ECLA, but few dispute the opinion that Prebisch's ideas gave the ECLA intellectual focus and spurred talented men and women to action. The ECLA had an organizational ideology--and it is generally acknowledged that an organizational ideology channels energy into purposeful action. The ECA has never had such an ideology. During his long tenure as head of the ECA, Robert Gardiner used his energy to conduct a wide range of studies, to seek the support and confidence of African leaders, and above all to gain his organization a reputation for seriousness and moderation. What his leadership lacked was the ability to organize his staff around a set of ideas and purposes, to make the ECA distinctive, or to publicize throughout Africa the actual or potential work of the organization. The ECA has still not developed the kind of identifiable personality that can make an impression on ideas and directions for development in Africa.

Even those who know of the ECA's varied activities criticize it for the unevenness of its work. One frequently hears the complaint that the specialized agencies--whatever their faults--can count among their staff a large number of high-caliber specialists, but that the ECA's staff is largely made up of generalists; the ECA provides neither the ideas of a think-tank, nor the expertise of a specialized agency. Thus, African states are prone to condemn the ECA not just as an arm of the UN, but as a particularly useless one.

When we look at the UN system in general and the ECA in particular, it seems unlikely that the ECA has, or can develop, the management capacity for handling Africa-directed aid in general; nor can it compete with the specialized agencies in their fields. Thus, the ECA's mission ought to be the development of inter-African enterprises. It might concentrate on regional and subregional activities, and whenever such projects and programs are proposed it should be the ECA, rather than a specialized agency, that is charged with their coordination and supervision. Defining the ECA's mission in this way is consistent with the organization's long-standing preference for multi-national activities and organizations--and gives the ECA a personality distinct from the UN system.

By 1975, the two most often heard suggestions for the future direction of the ECA were: 1) that it should reinvigorate itself through 'action programs,' and 2) that is should specialize in matters pertaining to more than one African state. The two suggestions are not incompatible. The ECA's past success and failures take on more significance in one's assessment of its present capacity if one is willing to make certain assumptions: 1) that the desirability of inter-African cooperation and integration will increase in years to come; 2) that the present stage of African economic development makes a number of inter-African cooperative efforts more rational (and hence more politically affordable) than was the case 10 or 15 years ago; 3) that African statesmen have gained a good deal of experience and have developed a pragmatism regarding inter-African enterprises; 4) that self-reliance and a new international economic order will both be easier to achieve if Africans are in the habit of collective economic and political action; 5) that supportive institutional mechanisms are desirable, both for facilitating collective action and for reversing the increasingly dismal economic situations in most small, poorly-endowed African countries; and 6) that it is more useful to try to reinvigorate the ECA, given its capacity to draw on international funds and its not inconsiderable experience, than to start over with a new organization.

African governments have made it clear, by their support of the Africanization of the ECA, that they believe in principle in a Regional Commission for Africa--as long as it is mainly directed by Africans. The current fashion of focusing on global economic restructuring and on the development of national capacities does not lessen, in the eyes of African governments, the desirability of having an effective arm of the United Nations system fully devoted to African development. The circumstances are propitious for the ECA; it is time for it to develop a focus and a mission--and an organizational structure appropriate to these. It might be of some interest meanwhile if we take a look at the ECA's achievements to date, and assess its current capacity and potential based on its work programs.

NOTES

1. The Author interviewed officials at the State Department and AID on the subject in 1965, 66, and 69.

2. From an interview with Adedeji quoted in <u>Africa</u>, No. 71, July, 1977, p. 49.

3 E/CN.14/WP 61 and M70-2480.

4. <u>Ibid</u>.

5 Aaron Wildavsky, <u>The Politics of the Budgetary Process</u>, Boston: Little Brown and Co., 1964, p. 1.

6. UN ECA 1976-77 Program Budget, M75-317.

7. Bilateral sources had been confined to industrial societies until 1977, when Adedeji called a conference of ECA members and asked for individual African commitments to ECA's budget. By July, 1977, 15 African countries pledged nearly $4 million for the 1976-81 work program. The pledges followed a meeting in Lagos in April, 1977, where member nations were asked to participate more directly in the ECA in the name of increased self-reliance and to accelerate African economic integration. The 15 countries who have pledged monies so far are: Benin, Central Africa Empire, Ethiopia, Liberia, Mauritius, Nigeria, Rwanda, Senegal, Sierra Leone, the Sudan, Tanzania, Uganda, Upper Volta, Zaire, Zambia. Nigeria gave the largest pledge so far ($1.6 million), followed

by Upper Volta with $819,206 and Tanzania with $150,000. This information is from <u>West Africa</u>, July 25, 1977, p. 1545.

8. E/CN.14/ECO/83.

9. <u>Ibid</u>., ECO/83, p. 1-5.

10. E/CN.14/INR/215, p. 12.

11. Mahbub ul Haq "Rich and Poor Nations," <u>Christian Science Monitor</u>, August 29, 1975, p. 14.

12. ECA/OAU (E/CN.14/649), 26 January 1976.

13. <u>Ibid</u>., p. 2.

14. <u>Ibid</u>., p. 9.

15. <u>Ibid</u>., p. 7.

16. Author's interview with A.M. Nakamura, Acting Chief of Industrial Section, at ECA Headquarters 3/18/76. Mr. Nakamura was acting as chief after the permanent chief of the division, an African, was unexpectedly recalled by his government. Mr. Nakamura had been with ECA for 4 years; prior to this he had been in the import-export business in Japan. I sensed that Mr. Nakamura might have liked to become permanent chief of his division, but thought his prospects non-existent since he was not African. Mr. Nakamura, given his somewhat unique national and professional background within ECA, was impressed by two things. First, that African countries needed 'packaged' aid money: financial aid, technology, management aid and salesmanship training had to go hand-in-hand in order to produce industrial development. Second, he noted that bilaterally-funded officials at ECA had travel money and could therefore visit countries and projects which they thought essential, while ECA regular staff had no such funds. As a consequence he thought bilaterally funded staff tended to be more useful, but since it takes 3-4 years to see a project through and bilateral people rarely stay that long, their usefulness was undermined.

17. ECA Revised Medium Term Plan for 1976-81 (ECN/TECO/31/Rev 1, May 10, 1976).

18. <u>Ibid</u>., TECO/31, p. 37.

19. <u>Ibid</u>., TECO/31, p. 37-38.

20. <u>Ibid</u>., TECO/31, p. 42.

21. <u>Ibid</u>., TECO/31, p. 80.

22. E/CN.14/ECO INF/34, p. 3.

23. GA Official Records. Thirty First Session Supplement No. 34 (A/31/34), p. 6.

24. <u>Ibid</u>., p. 13.

25. <u>Ibid</u>., p. 13.

26. The new organization of ECA. Became effective mid-1976.

27. E/CN.14/ECO/INF/34 Rev 1, 15 April 1976.

28. E/CN.14/424, p. 178.

29. E/CN.14/664, p. 5.

30. Interview with Adedeji in *Africa*, *op. cit.*, No. 71, 1977, p. 49.

31. E/CN 14/644, *op. cit.*, p. 5.

# 4
# ECA's Activities and Work Programs

## INTRODUCTION

From an observer's point of view, the ECA's activities and work programs appear to fall into three categories. The first category includes activities characteristic of a member of the international development assistance community; the ECA takes on these activities as an institutional arm of the United Nations system. Such activities, whether they be national, regional or continental, are intended to speed African development. Generating a data base for development, undertaking feasibility studies for projects or programs, rendering technical assistance, engaging in manpower training, and serving as a consultant, all fall into this first category. While these activities are clearly within the ECA's mandate as a UN Regional Commission, similar activities have been, and still are, carried out at the same time by other agencies of the UN in their operations in Africa. The ECA, in its position as a regional arm of the UN, clearly perceives one of its functions to be the general upgrading of the continent's capacity for development; but so far the ECA has merely overlapped or competed with the rest of the international development assistance community in general (and the UN specialized agencies in particular) in participating in the activities falling under this category.

The second category of ECA activities is defined by the ECA's role as a builder of African inter-state institutions. The ECA has, in accepting its mandate as an African regional institution, dedicated itself to fostering the establishment of African inter-state regional and subregional institutions. African and international interest in such institutions in the 1960s, combined with Robert Gardiner's firm belief that African development called for inter-state cooperation and integration, caused the ECA to channel many of its activities into this category. It undertook background studies, set up conferences, worked out charters and in general played the midwife to such inter-state institutions as the African Development Bank, the West African Currency Clearing House, various river and lake commissions, and the recently-formed Economic Community of West African States (ECOWAS). Like the ECLA, the ECA believed that it had a special mission to foster regionalism and to facilitate in any way it could the establishment of inter-state institutions with cooperative and/or integrative possibilities.

Activities falling into the third category are those concerning the ECA's efforts to develop regional and subregional subsidiaries of its secretariat. The ECA sought to expand its own institutional structure in order to become the organizational core around which African integration and cooperation could be established. The ECA set up its own subregional offices, which in addition to providing this organizational core, were to facilitate the ECA's work in categories one and two. We will see later that as the 1960s wore on, the ECA's attempts to establish itself as the institutional nucleus for African regional integration became less energetic; it turned its attention to emphasizing inter-state cooperation instead.

In spite of a certain amount of overlap among the three categories, it is useful to look at each category as representing a different set of organizational purposes and capabilities. By engaging in all three categories of activities at once, the ECA was interpreting its dual mandate in the widest possible fashion.

This chapter will explore the ECA's activities under each of these categories. It seeks to show how the ECA's efforts to undertake activities in all three categories, and to fulfill both terms of its dual mandate, generated problems for the organization.

## CATEGORY I - THE ECA AS AN ARM OF THE INTERNATIONAL DEVELOPMENT ASSISTANCE COMMUNITY: INCREASING AFRICAN NATIONAL AND REGIONAL DEVELOPMENT CAPACITIES

### Data Collection and Dissemination

One of the handicaps afflicting all African governments on the eve of independence was the appalling lack of appropriate statistical and other data necessary for national and regional development planning. The old colonial regimes had collected quantities of statistics, but their data was more relevant to trade and colonial control than to state development. Population figures, social statistics, resource and production data were all in short supply. There was no continent-wide data collection and dissemination mechanism that inter-African planners could use. The ECA saw it as one of its first tasks to organize, generate and distribute the sort of data that any national and inter-African planning required.[1]

Today relatively reliable African statistical information is published regularly, and is used with relative confidence both inside and outside Africa; the ECA s achievements in this field are widely acknowledged. Not only is vital information now available in many areas of state and interstate planning, but procedures and a mechanism have been established for supplying national statistical information to ECA-supervised collection and publication facilities. As a consequence, inter-state cooperation in this field has led to a regularization of procedures, training of skilled statisticians, and the establishment of national statistical services where none had existed before or where the ones that did exist needed to be improved.

There is still a good deal of unevenness in this field; national capacities are still not consistently good. Small least-developed countries tend to have the least-developed statistical services. In addition, data which governments must generate for themselves, such as household information, is still very poorly developed. In 1974, the ECA tried to identify some of the problems of collecting statistics at the national level--the time lag between a request for statistics and a governmental response at times exceeded the accepted two or three months. If found, for example, that there continued to be divisions between English- and French-speakers; the English-speaking countries used the UN system of national accounts, but the French-speaking countries still did not. The mending of this division is important not only from the standpoint of uniform statistics-gathering, but also from that of inter-African cooperation and planning. Still, most would agree that the ECA has made impressive achievements in this field in the last 20 years.[2]

There are, besides statistics, other fields of data collection and dissemination that deserve our attention. There have recently been a number of calls for the development of regional data banks,[3] and the whole UN system is at work, along with the Statistical Divisions of the Regional Commissions, on developing useable data services--that is, services that can be easily used at both the national and international levels. In many areas of knowledge, including the all-important one of appropriate technology, information dissemination facilities in Africa are very poor indeed. The ECA could play just as important a role in the development of data banks and dissemination procedures as it did in the field of generating statistics. However, the ECA has done little to establish itself as a resource center; nor has it developed other resource centers on the African continent. The ECA library, potentially one such center, is of such poor quality that it is of little use to anyone. Other UN facilities, such as the UNEP or the UNESCO Science and Technology Library in Nairobi, are equally inadequate, even in their limited specialties. There are various other libraries, as well as health and technology demonstration centers, strewn across the continent--few of which are as effective as they could be. Rationalizing this network of data facilities in order to make better use of existing development information is a task that urgently needs to be done; furthermore, it is one that would be appropriate to the ECA's self-defined mission.

National and regional development planning in the 1960s was often based on what one UN official termed "inspired guesses." Planning today proceeds on much firmer ground, but still without the accumulation of data customary in development planning in industrial countries.

In the 1960s African states had little access to that data and information, available in the industrial world, that would be of use to development planners in Africa (i.e., technology, agriculture, human and animal health). It is in this area of giving Africa access to international data resources that regional and subregional data banks would be most useful

Furthermore, a regional organization that has access to international data sources and that is capable of collecting and distributing national and regional data could play an exceedingly important role within the context of the NIEO. Africa's collective ability to exert leverage on its own behalf in the international system, and to speak with authority regarding its individual and collective needs, is heavily dependent on its having a well-organized data collection. The ECA's role in acquiring for Africa this collection of data, while relatively unknown and unappreciated, is one of the organization's greatest contributions to date; it provides a service unmatched by any other mechanism on the continent.

## Manpower Training: Workshops and Seminars

Raising Africa's skilled manpower capacity at all levels of society was one of the most pressing tasks facing African states in the post-independence decade. Many of these states became independent with only a handful of university graduates among their citizenry. Even those countries with a larger number of university-trained citizens, such as Ghana and Nigeria, found that they were lacking nationals trained in certain technical fields (medicine, engineering, industrial and agricultural development). All African countries had, moreover, acute shortages of middle-level administrators to carry out the day-to-day work of governing while national economies were being developed. Accountants and office managers were in as short supply as agricultural extension workers, road engineers, or nurses. In fact, Africa's skilled manpower shortage was one of the greatest barriers to translating political independence into other forms of independence, and to transforming externally-generated economic aid into national development and self-reliance. Without their own administrators and technicians, African countries will continue to be dependent on forces outside of Africa, be they industrial societies, multinational corporations, or international agencies. An NIEO that produces additional capital resources for African states will only benefit those states that have the manpower to turn capital resources into economic and social development of their own societies.

Given the vastness of Africa's skilled manpower problems, the ECA's activities in this field are bound to appear minimal. Manpower training is itself a complex subject which, even for the purposes of analysis, is heavily dependent on a working knowledge of one's needs and goals; but few African states have undertaken careful studies of their current and future manpower needs. Even those governments that do generate manpower figures in a certain field frequently do so less on the basis of careful national study than out of a need to meet the demands of an insistent international agency. In addition, because manpower shortages in all fields are so vast, individuals trained in a certain field are often given administrative or political duties unrelated to their special technical training. In short, the problem is so vast and the subject so complex that it is really no wonder that an organization like the ECA finds it difficult to address the issue.

Manpower development suffers particularly when an organization's programs and priorities are as ill-focused as the ECA's have often been. As in other areas, the ECA's fuzzy image as an African organization has failed to convince its clients that there are certain tasks that the ECA can and ought to carry out in this field. And of course the ECA's uncertain position within the UN structure has left it unclear as to what its manpower training role ought to be in the presence of the other UN agencies operating on the African continent (ILO, UNESCO, FAO). The way the ECA has handled Africa's urgent need for manpower training is illustrative of its difficulty in focusing on an issue, and exposes its split personality and lack of coherent planning.

The ECA's activities in the manpower training field came under attack in a 1970 team of experts' report on the organization's training program. Prior to becoming the ECA's executive secretary, Adebayo Adedeji was a member of that team.[4] The evaluation group found unanimous agreement among African government officials (and among UN officials in the field) that there are far too many ECA-sponsored manpower training seminars, workshops, and conferences. ECA activities in this field were said to be too varied to make any lasting impact; furthermore, competition among the UN agencies caused duplication of efforts and waste of personnel[5]--which is not surprising, since UN agencies rarely consult with one another. The team was surprised to discover, for example, that the ECA/FAO joint division in Addis Ababa had no direct responsibility for training in its field (agriculture), and that neither the FAO's regional office in Accra nor its headquarters in Rome consulted with the ECA on the courses they planned for Africa.[6] In addition, governments frequently did not receive notice in sufficient time to avail themselves of an opportunity to send nationals to conferences and workshops. But the blame for the largely unsatisfactory handling of training courses and seminars deserves to be shared; most African governments have not established priorities and targets for their manpower needs. Hence it is left for the ECA and other agencies to determine what training course priorities should be.

Still the report places the burden of blame largely on the shoulders of the ECA; the evaluation team declared that "it is virtually a misnomer" to call the ECA program of work and priorities a 'program,' since "a 'program' implies a closely interrelated series of activities and projects, all of whose primary aim is to achieve a given overall goal or objective, or a series of goals and objectives." The report went on to say that "A program would also indicate the strategy for achieving such goals, and the priority ratings of the various activities."[7] The evaluation team found in 1970 (as did this observer during interviews in 1976) little evidence that the ECA had stated goals and objectives that informed its planning of workshops and seminars; nor did the cumulative effect of the seminars carried out over the years reflect an unstated goal or objective.[8] As a consequence, African governments, other agencies, and the ECA are all engaged in random activities in the training field, and both the subject matter and the participants of these activities are frequently left to accidents of chance. If the ECA were just another UN agency in Africa, it could not be blamed for this; but since it perceives of itself as a focal point for UN activities in Africa, a much harsher judgment of its achievements in the training of manpower is appropriate.

*Ad hoc* conferences with varied degrees of participation by nationals from member countries have made an uncertain impact. I have mentioned that the need for middle-grade personnel in Africa is considerable. In the past, both the ECA and many African countries favored regional and subregional training sessions as a way of meeting this need. Now, however, the cost of sending a sizable contingent of nationals to a conference seems excessive. As a consequence, there is an increasing tendency to prefer training at the national level, and at the subregional level only when necessary. Under these circumstances, both the ECA and the governments involved are forced to clarify their own needs and goals--for unless they do so, genuinely beneficial training courses will never be held.

It is evident that a costly all-out attack on Africa's serious manpower shortage will require resources not currently available (either from the UN or from African countries) to the ECA. In addition, no manpower program will be successful until the problem of overlapping and competing UN agencies is solved. However, there is one thing the ECA can do with the financial and human resources it has right now: develop the goals and objectives that the evaluation team found wanting. Once a framework for reorganization and increased effort can be set up, it will be easier to gain additional resources and to encourage member government support.

The emphasis of this discussion so far has been on the failures of the ECA's attempts to hold meetings, workshops, and training courses that could be of some use to its clients. The main criticism leveled against the ECA is that it has not developed a program that rationalizes all these activities--and that as a consequence, its services in this area are of uneven quality. However, the ECA's performance has not been uniformly poor. Indeed the ECA's training sessions have provided what little training has been available to Africans in a number of fields; it helped publicize the importance of middle-level manpower training, for instance, at a time (early- and mid-'60s) when middle-level administrators and support personnel were given low priority, both by African governments and by international donors.

While its past work and current capacity are justifiably criticized, the ECA has nevertheless tried to address itself to the shifting needs and concerns of Africans; it has often possessed know-how not made available to Africans through their governments or through other inter-African institutions.

In addition, by combining its data collection and research facilities with its conference and training activities, the ECA has been able to represent its clients' needs and priorities in the international community. In the 1960s, for example, the ECA began to take an interest in integrated rural development. Conferences were convened, manpower and technology problems were studied, reports were written, and manpower training sessions were held. The ECA gathered enough information through these activities to make effective appeals to the UN system and bilateral donors for technical assistance. The ECA's efforts, though lacking in coordination, served at least to identify needs; at times it was able to meet those needs by obtaining resources from the international system. Though the ECA lacked an identifiable ideology, it was still able to serve its clients by generating a data base, identifying needs producing studies, and undertaking training activities; it influenced development priorities and generated international resources in spite of its chronic inability to coordinate its own activities. Today, the ECA's experience in, and abilities to build conference and training institutions on an inter-African basis still exceed that of any other continental organization in Africa. More importantly, the ECA's random activities in the manpower training field, and the complaints it has received about them, have led to the kind of critical evaluation that has made possible new approaches to the problem--the kind of evaluation that the ECA would do well to undertake in other areas.

One consequence of this evaluation has been a move away from *ad hoc* training activities and towards development of regional centers. Regional centers are meant to combine research and training in areas where national need is great but where the human and capital resources available make a regional solution more feasible. On the other hand, the ECA has also come to realize that *ad hoc* regional and subregional training workshops (especially for middle-level personnel) are inefficient, and that while some high-power training ought to be offered through regional institutions, other types of manpower training ought to be offered locally by the states. A training course for accountants might be run more effectively and economically if the ECA simply made resources and technical assistance available to, say, Tanzania, rather than ask 25 Tanzanians to travel all the way to Addis Ababa or Accra for a training workshop.

These changes will increasingly make it possible to localize manpower training on the one hand, and to establish permanent regional institutions on the other hand. It is too early to tell what effects these changes will have; however, certain improvements are already discernible. The establishment of regional research and training centers reduces the number of Africans who have to be trained overseas, thus cutting down costs and avoiding the risk that overseas training will turn out to be inappropriate or lead to a brain drain. Research and training institutions should also make it possible for Africa's manpower capability to advance at the same rate as its technology in any given field. So a social welfare center can study African social welfare problems, then use its findings as the basis for training decision-making personnel in that field. Similarly, localizing most of the lower level training at the national level allows African states to use external resources for increasing their national capacities. In addition, training people at the national level allows for greater national participation and commitment to the enterprise. In short, it looks as though the establishment of regional centers coupled with the use of international resources to increase manpower capacity at the national level, is a promising reform in the ECA's human resources program; the ECA remains the only organization in Africa that is in a position to make a success of these enterprises.

However, there remains a key unresolved issue in the manpower field: overlap and competition among the various UN agencies. UNESCO, ILO, and FAO all engage in activities similar to those of the ECA. African governments and inter-state organizations are frequently hard put to know which UN agency can best serve their needs.

Valuable international resources are wasted, of course, when duplication of effort and lack of coordination take place among international agencies. Thus in the area of manpower training, as in so many other areas, the ECA's role as a Regional Commission and its relationship to the other UN agencies still require clarification.

## Consultants

I have mentioned that a sizable component of the ECA's supplemental income that is derived from bilateral and multi-lateral sources goes toward employing experts and consultants.[9] Some of these individuals join the ECA's secretariat staff at headquarters; others are sent to serve a member government; still others are attached to inter-governmental institutions or are designated as roving regional advisors for the continent. Of course, the ECA's regular budget also includes funding for consultants; its regular staff includes experts in statistics and population planning, as well as consultants trained in specific areas of industry, agriculture, and education--to name a few. Due to the small (relative to Africa's vast needs) scale of its operations, the ECA's activities in this field often appear to be undertaken purely at random. However, within the context of its limited resources, the ECA has always tried to designate priority areas (e.g., population planning, integrated rural development, appropriate technology) and to equip itself with a regional consultant for each. Such experts are available to member countries and their inter-state institutions, and are also available to ECA headquarters for help in formulating programs and projects.

One highly-placed ECA official once pointed out (in another context) that one of the largest invisible drains on African economies is their huge investment, which has never been accurately calculated, in foreign consultants. Without going into a discussion of the uneven quality of advice rendered to African countries by consultants from industrial states, one must agree that the extraordinary costs African states pay for these services demand that another way be found for them to obtain development expertise.

The ECA's long-term objective in this field, then, is the training of African manpower in those areas where at this time only foreign consultants are available. In the interim, the problem is how to increase the quality and accessibility of consultancy services. The African states' need for consultants and advisors is one area which calls for immediate regional action--especially if the utilization of newly-available resources from an NIEO is to be determined by African governments rather than by external forces.

In the 1970s and '80s it is reasonable to suppose that African national development, together with the capacities of African inter-state institutions and the ECA, will make it feasible to offer vastly increased consultancy services on a regional or subregional basis. The establishment of such services would insure better utilization of available African expertise; it would also lower the cost and raise the efficiency of (and ECA control over) the experts supported by multilateral and bilateral funds. Unless more such services are made available, African regional and national development will continue to be at the mercy of random public efforts and private enterprises. While the problems African states face in this area are immense, and the achievements of the ECA so far seem minimal, the ECA's efforts over the last 20 years have gained it the experience and institutional capacity to effect changes in the years to come.

## CATEGORY II - THE ECA AS A BUILDER OF AFRICAN INTER-STATE INSTITUTIONS

The ECA has established, or helped to establish, a wide range of inter-African institutions.* We will recall that from its very inception, the ECA operated on the assumption that African development and African self-reliance required regional institutional arrangements; its documents over the years are filled with exhortations to build inter-state institutions. The ECA received international verbal support for its studies advocating inter-African institution-building, but due to countervailing forces (especially of an economic kind), it received little material

It received even less political support from African states throughout most of the 1960s.

---

*See appendix IV.

Many of the more radical African states were committed to continental unification, and believed that subregional arrangements would undermine it. The majority of African states paid lip service to ECA proposals, but believed, for very good reasons, that there was no visible and immediate advantage in following through on ECA recommendations for institution-building.[10]

In spite of these obstacles, the ECA continued its campaign by doing studies on inter-African institutional arrangements and by setting up meetings between relevant nationals. As we shall see, the ECA's achievements in this field have not been spectacular, but the efforts have increasingly made an impact on the thinking about regional arrangements. It is unfortunate that political and economic realities in Africa were not conducive to multinational institutions when the ECA first advocated them; however, African states are now beginning to see that national self-interest *can* be served by regional arrangements. Because of the slow pace of regional integration and the number of words that have preceded any action, critics are still prone to underrate the ECA s role in this field. However, as the cases I will cite will illustrate, the ECA's effectiveness in this area, when viewed over a period of 20 years, has been considerable.

Between 1958 and 1968, the ECA organized and supervised nearly 200 multi-state conferences; since 1968, it has held more than twice that many. On a continent as large, as heterogeneous, and as ill-equipped for inter-state communications as Africa, bringing leaders together to discuss subjects of mutual interest is an important service; inter-state cooperation requires inter-state relationships among relevant officials. By offering these multi-state conferences, the ECA helped establish continental cooperative patterns, and contributed to African development.

It is of course difficult to gauge the worth of the ECA contribution in this area. The ECA has generally played the role of generating interest among member states in inter-African cooperation, and of making available it own expertise in the area; its basic assumption has been that the most important thing it can do for the vast African continent is to encourage the exchange of ideas among states and the undertaking of inter-state cooperative action. Since neither African development nor regional integration has progressed quickly enough for most actors and observers, it is tempting to conclude that the ECA s activities have all been failures. However, it is still useful to examine the ECA's limited contributions in order to better understand the obstacles to, and possibilities for, inter-state institution-building in Africa.

It might be best to start with a discussion of the impact of these conferences and meetings, some of which resulted in the establishment of inter-African organizations. In the spring of 1976, for example, the ECA played host at a meeting at ECA headquarters to establish an African Regional Standards Organization. The objectives of this organization are "to promote social, industrial, and economic development, and to provide protection and human safety, by advocating and establishing activities which would enable African countries to harmonize their views and to create better facilities for international exchange of goods and for import replacement in particular. The hope is that such an organization will facilitate trade among African countries and promote intra-African cooperation."[11] The founding meeting for the standards organization was scheduled for 1977.

The ECA has for a number of years engaged in activities related to a standards organization. For an earlier meeting (September 1975) it provided a draft constitution based on the constitution of the International Organization for Standardization (ISO). Until the African standards organization takes up its duties, an ECA *ad hoc* inter-divisional committee on standardization will continue to provide assistance and information. This is a typical process; meetings are held to identify the need for an organization or institution, rules and procedures are drafted, more meetings are held to consider amendments and to consult with the ECA, and the ECA continues to give aid and advice until the organization is launched. The propitiousness of developing a standards organization is now apparent to African leaders, making such an enterprise feasible; in the 1960s, efforts would have been premature and fruitless. Thus, the success of an ECA organizational conference can be measured by its end product--a working inter-governmental organization or arrangement that speeds the process of African development.

A similar process can be seen in the establishment of inter-African financial and monetary institutions. When the ECA came into existence in 1958, most African countries were largely dependent on their former colonizers, and were part of the colonizers' monetary zones. Few African countries (Morocco was an exception) had central banks until the middle 1950s. An African state's trade relations were tied up with those of a former metropolitan power, making it difficult to form other external ties--especially between neighboring countries who belonged to different monetary zones. (This helps explain why in West Africa in particular there was little economic intercourse among neighbors before independence.)

Some of the ECA's earliest studies deal with African capital accumulation. By its third session in 1961, the ECA had included in its work program the establishment of an African Development Bank (Res. 27/III), as well as studies of African monetary systems within the context of promoting intra-African trade and economic development (Res. 30/III). At its fourth session the following year, it presented a study on the establishment of an African Development Bank.[12] In July and August of 1963, African finance ministers met in Khartoum; in the same year all member states were urged to participate in a conference at which an agreement for the establishment of the Development Bank was approved. The agreement was made available for member states' ratification in August, 1964, and it went into effect that September; the first meeting of the Bank's Board of Governors took place in Lagos on November 4. (Permanent headquarters for the Bank were later established in Abidjan, the capital of the Ivory Coast.) The African Development Bank took more time than expected in coming to play an important role in Africa, but its establishment was an impressive achievement for the ECA, which pursued this objective with great resolve even while it was still in its formative years.[13]

By now, the African Development Bank (or ADB) has become an important regional institution, one which performs a number of functions besides acquiring capital for development purposes. The Bank has worked with other African institutions (including the ECA) and international organizations to promote--through funding, preparatory work, and technical support--African cooperation in such matters as telecommunications and road construction. Unlike the Asian Development Bank, the ADB has limited its membership to states on its own continent--losing the benefit of having affluent industrial states among its members, but gaining the advantage of being identified as an African organization. (Non-African states are allowed, however, to participate in the African Development Fund, established in 1966.)

The ECA also developed early an interest in facilitating inter-African financial transactions. In 1963, during its fifth session, it decided to study the possibility of establishing a currency clearing system, as part of a payments union for African countries.[14] The possibility of creating a compensation and payments union was also studied.[15] Studies and reports followed, each of which indicated an awareness of the intimate relationship between a clearing system, the formation of regional and subregional economic communities, and the development of trade ties among African countries. The complexity of the subject required additional studies on other aspects of ordering African economic life: one study examined bilateral trade and payments agreements, while another looked into the balance-of-payments problems of African countries. The ECA also held seminars and training sessions dealing with financial matters: in 1965 it offered an advanced seminar in Current Problems and Training Needs in Tax Administration,[16] and later (among others) held sessions on Budget Planning and Management. The ECA acquired a good deal of information in the process, and was able to give Africans instruction both on the issues and on their roles in national and regional development.

The lasting effect of various conferences and reports is that appropriate machinery can be assembled as soon as member states desire it--precious time and enthusiasm are not lost during a lengthy study period, since the studying has already been done by the ECA. Two examples of this come to mind: the establishment of the Association of African Central Banks, and the agreement to establish a West African Clearing House.

In 1966, African development had reached a point where a meeting of the Governors of the various African Central Banks seemed appropriate.

Only a few years earlier, the Governors themselves might have justifiably considered such a meeting a waste of time. Following this meeting, an interim committee of representatives from the ADB, IDEP and the ECA prepared a statute for an Association of Central Banks; in 1968 this statute was adopted.[17] Here too one might argue that an Association of Central Banks is hardly a revolution in development thinking, but institutional arrangements and channels of communication make up the infrastructure of African development and inter-African cooperation.

A slightly different illustration is that of the drafting of an agreement for a West African Clearing House to facilitate "multilateral settlements among the banks of the West African subregion." The agreement set out the objectives of the clearing house:

> to promote the use of the currencies of the members of the Clearing House for sub-regional trade and other transactions;
>
> to bring about economies in the use of foreign reserves of the members of the Clearing House;
>
> to encourage the members of the Clearing House to liberalize trade among their respective countries; and
>
> to promote monetary cooperation and consulting members of the Clearing House.[18]

The draft for this agreement was prepared by the ECA in response to requests from the countries concerned, but the history of ECA studies, suggestions, and proddings about the desirability of clearing houses, at least on subregional levels goes back for years; a clearing house is obviously a prerequisite to developing an Economic Community. However, subregional mechanisms were not perceived by member governments as necessary ten years ago, and it was not until 1976 that they considered a clearing house important enough to ask the ECA to help establish one. This change of opinion is not due merely to the increased wisdom or enlightenment of West African leaders, but rather to the fact that intercourse between West African states has become frequent enough for West African economists and politicians to justify forming such a mechanism. The recognition of a need for, and the progress made so far in establishing, a West African Clearing House illustrates the fact that components of European-derived integration theories of the 1950s and '60s are receiving serious consideration and support in the '70s and '80s, now that Africans themselves are perceiving the utility of certain types of inter-state institutions.

As it did with other inter-state institutions, the ECA played the role of a midwife in the birth of the West African Clearing House. The ECA was what kept the subject alive; it made feasibility studies, did the preparatory work, and, by issuing documents and holding conferences, convinced the appropriate African officials of the potential utility of such a regional mechanism. The ECA had the ideological commitment and the resources to do this background work. It also had the staff required to draft an agreement that could serve as the blue print, if not the final constitution of an African regional arrangement.

From the perspective of the West African states, as well as from that of the ECA, a clearing house was essential to the successful operation of the Economic Community of West African States (ECOWAS). (ECA experts also made a substantial contribution to the drafting of the ECOWAS treaty, which owes much to the Treaty of Rome, and to the Lome Convention between EEC and ACP states.) The ECOWAS treaty itself and the plan for gradual integration of ECOWAS member states (which is to take place over a period of 15 years) are specially tailored to suit the needs, both economic and political, of ECOWAS members. One can see that under some circumstances the ECA's advocacy of, and organizational capacity to promote regional institutions manages to coincide with African states' recognition that such institutions might serve their needs. Efforts to develop African subregional communities prior to any substantial interaction among African states were clearly premature. Within the context of increased West African inter-state relations, the ECA, with its expertise in preparatory work for inter-state institution-building, can render its clients a valuable service and can make a real contribution to inter-African cooperation.

It is useful to note that the past two decades have witnessed concrete changes on the African continent of the sort that increase the desirability of inter-state institution-building in a number of economic areas. At the same time, lessons learned from the malfunctioning of so many regional mechanisms in the 1960s are now helping the ECA and its member states to approach regional institution-building with a good deal more sophistication. African states are no longer merely imitating the regional arrangements of the industrial societies, but are basing African institutions on those in other parts of the Third World (e.g., Latin America), and on their own experiences on the African continent. For example, the ECOWAS protocol concerned with the complex question of 'the definition of the origin of products' comes almost word-for-word from the Lome Convention. This borrowing of solutions to similar problems allows African states to profit from each other's experience, and speeds the development of workable institutional arrangements. African negotiators and the ECA advisory staff have also begun to exchange knowledge. In short, the sophistication the ECA has gained in the last decade, combined with member states' changed perceptions of the usefulness of such arrangements, now makes possible a number of regional arrangements prematurely advocated by the ECA and others in the 1960s.

## CATEGORY III - THE ROLE OF THE ECA'S SUBSIDIARY INSTITUTIONS

In this section I will examine the ECA's efforts to become Africa's main regional and subregional mechanism. I do not refer here to the ECA's efforts to help member states establish regional institutions, but rather to its efforts to set out extensions of itself that would allow it to play a more immediate role in African regional cooperation and integration. Such subregional extensions are consistent with the ECA's UN mandate, which envisions it as an African continental organization intended to foster regionalism; however, such extensions put the ECA in a position of competing with institutions initiated by its member states--and sometimes facilitated by the ECA itself. For example, in its efforts to establish a subregional office in East Africa that would serve as a focal point for East African regional integration, the ECA came into the con flict with the already-existing East African Common

Services Organization, which was seeking to serve the same purpose. As we will see in the following pages, the potential conflict between the ECA's activities in Category II and those in Category III, while still unresolved, has nevertheless led the ECA to redefine its goals and to alter its perception of itself as the central institution in any multi-state economic community.

## ECA Subregional Offices

Due to the size of the African continent and the great number of African states, the ECA decided in the early 1960s that its work could be made easier if it established subregional offices. Such offices, it assumed, could also serve as the nuclei for integrated subregional communities. The ECA accordingly set up four subregional offices: one in Kinshasa, in the former Congo to serve Central Africa; one in Tangier, Morocco to serve North Africa; one in Lusaka, Zambia to serve East Africa; and one in Niamey Niger to serve West Africa.

ECA documents from the 1960s imply that the four regional offices were intended not merely to aid ECA headquarters in its work, but also to provide a subregional coordinating mechanism for the activities of all the UN agencies in the area.

It can be argued that while subregional offices were consistent with the 1960s assumption that regional integration in Africa was desirable and feasible, the ECA's attempts to establish such offices (and the dual functions it assigned them) were manifestations of its split personality. In this respect as in so many others, it was trying to be both an extension of the UN and an African organization; the ECA genuinely believed that its mission was to provide a focal point for subregional institution-building.

Since the ECA was trying to support other African regional integration efforts at the same time that it was establishing these offices, it was in a sense competing with itself. Thus, the regional offices frequently failed to gain the attention and support of states in the region, who were often preoccupied with the establishment or ongoing operations of other subregional institutions. In addition, the ECA's disabilities--bureaucratic weakness at headquarters, shortages of staff--also afflicted the subregional offices. It is fair to say that the offices were failures in all three respects: they did not provide focal points for regional integration efforts, they did not become working extension bureaus of ECA headquarters and they did not have any success in coordinating UN activities in Africa.

Rather than being formally abandoned, these regional offices were gradually supplanted by other institutional mechanisms, although the ECA still considers subregional institutional structures appropriate to fulfillment of its mandate. There was a period in the early 1970s when the UN Multi-disciplinary Development Advisory Teams (UNDATs) briefly engaged the attention of both UN and ECA headquarters; UNDATs were in some cases located in the same place as the regional offices (e.g., Niamey and Lusaka) and were intended to work closely with them. While the UNDATs did not exactly replace the regional offices, they did help both the UN and the ECA redefine their thinking with regard to the development of the ECA's subregional institutions.

## The United Nations Multidisciplinary Development Advisory Teams (UNDATs) and the United Nations Multinational Programming and Operational Centers (MULPOCs)

The UN recognized during the 1960s that it lacked coordination between agencies, as well as coordination between its own institutions and bilateral agencies. At the beginning of the Second Development Decade in the 1970s--the UN increasingly recognized that the LDCs needed help in establishing their own services for the planning and use of development aid. Therefore, the General Assembly created the Multidisciplinary Development Advisory Teams (UNDATs)[19] (or Multinational Programming and Operational Centers (MULPOCs), as they were renamed in 1977). The UN initially (1970) set up seven UNDATs, three of which were to be placed in Africa; in 1973 there were UNDATs in Yaounde and Niamey, and by 1974 there was another in Lusaka.

The UNDATs were not intended to take the place of the existing technical services offered by UN headquarters, the Specialized Agencies, or the ECA subregional offices. They were expected to supplement the work of these experts, but mostly they were to identify the need for, and implement, multinational projects, and identify national projects that could be multinationalized. The UNDATs were allowed a certain amount of flexibility so that it would be easier for them to work with a large number of governments, inter-governmental organizations, and UN Specialized Agencies.

The UNDATs were conceptualized as flexible task forces serving multinational interests. They were supposed to avoid getting caught up in the UN programs of any given country, and to concentrate on fostering multinational cooperation in such areas as transport, trade, and industry. By having a working knowledge of the problems of several states, an UNDAT would be in a position to suggest areas of cooperation; by drawing on the expertise of the ECA in addition to its own, an UNDAT could recommend sound solutions to problems.

The choices of team leaders for the African UNDATs were made jointly by the UN Department of Economic and Social Affairs in New York and the ECA. Team members were chosen by a similar procedure, but in order to insure smooth working conditions and a staff with complementary skills, the team leaders were consulted as well. The team leader had the responsibility for the day-to-day workings of the team; his position was one of potentially great authority and creativity. He was to coordinate the activities of UN agencies and bilateral donors, and to consult with the local Resident Representatives of the countries in his region. UNDAT team reports were to be sent to the Department of Economic and Social Affairs, the UNDP Resident Representative, and the governments concerned.

The United Nations financed the UNDATs partly through its regular budget and partly out of funds-in-trust deposited under bilateral agreements with interested governments. The UN also supplied experts and equipment for the teams. On a day-to-day basis, however, the management of the UNDATs in Africa was entrusted to the ECA. Thus the UNDATs, like the subregional offices, became a field arm of the ECA secretariat, and the two were supposed to be in regular communication. The UNDATs were meant to participate in the formulation and implementation of the ECA's work program, and were supposed to be able to go to the ECA's substantive divisions for backup work and expertise.[20] However, the UNDATs were also held responsible for their own regions.

Let us look, by way of illustration, at the Niamey UNDAT. At the beginning, its staff consisted of a transport economist, a mining expert, and the team leader. After doing some work with the ECA staff in the region, the UNDAT was assigned a general economist, a hydrologist, a human resources expert, a rural sociologist, and an assistant economist. At first the UNDAT offered advisory services to governments and intergovernmental organizations in the region. The transport economist undertook specific missions at the request of the Entente Council's Comite Superieur des Transports Terrestres (CSTT), the Lake Chad Basin Commission, and the Economic Community of West Africa (CEAO). These missions were related to plans for investment policy in transport development in Upper Volta and Niger, the transport problems of the CEAO, the creation of training institutions, and the transport difficulties of land-locked countries.[21]

The services rendered by the UNDAT helped strengthen existing intergovernmental machinery in the region, supplemented other UN activities, and benefited individual governments directly. The flexibility and mobility of the UNDAT did give it special advantages, but the small staff was entirely dependent on the quality of its individual expert in any given field. Besides carrying out advisory tasks, the mining expert and the hydrologist did studies of the mineral deposits on the borders of Togo and Benin (gold, phosphate, copper) and of Togo and Ghana (chromium). The team as a whole also participated in ILO and UNCTAD projects in the region; in 1974 the sociologist and the human resources expert worked with UNICEF on a study of the population movements, brought on by a drought in the Sahel, in Mali, Niger, Upper Volta, Mauritania, and Senegal. The economist produced some basic studies on the countries in his subregion and worked with an ECA advisor on a study of tourism in the Entente countries.[22]

The Lusaka UNDAT was meant to have 26 senior and 7 junior experts, but due to funding shortages (which began after it had been in operation a year) it was never assigned more than 12. Studies on transport in the region, rural development, and subregional trade have thus proceeded more slowly than planned.

These funding shortages were a result of the fact that no long-term financing arrangements were made for the UNDATs when they were established. At the outset, they were heavily dependent on bilateral support from such countries as the Netherlands, Sweden, and the United States. As I have mentioned, the UNDP funded the teams in 1976 while it and the ECA evaluated the teams' contributions. This joint evaluation recommended strongly that the UNDATs continue their work, and that three more teams be created to give Africa better coverage. The report also recommended that the teams' structural relationship to the ECA be changed; subsequently their work programs became more fully integrated into that of the ECA, hence the new name: Multinational Programming and Operational Centers (MULPOCs). This change made the teams the direct operational arms of the ECA. The evaluation study's recommendation that three centers be added was accepted, and plans are now being made to establish one for Central Africa, one for North Africa, and one for the coastal countries of West Africa (leaving the Niamey UNDAT able to concentrate on the Sahel countries).[23] (Unfortunately, the problem of financing has still not been resolved; hopes that early Africanization of the teams would convince African governments to take over the support of the MULPOCs have so far come to naught.)

One can see both problems and possibilities in the above description of the structure and staffing of the MULPOCs. MULPOCs are potentially very flexible instruments that could make realistic responses to African trends of the 1970s: that is, they can help with the kinds of inter-state activities that speed the development of integrated regional communities. MULPOCs appear to offer greater possibilities for inter-country planning and coordination.

In spite of efforts to spell out the MULPOCs' role, however, it is obvious that they have the potential to overlap, compete with, and duplicate the efforts of other agencies of the UN family. Communications between UN agencies are already poor; there is nothing to guarantee that the addition of the MULPOCs will make them any better. The creativity of the role a MULPOC will play cannot be determined structurally; as always, it is dependent on the quality and appropriateness of the members of its small staff. It is immensely difficult to recruit first-rate people who have appropriate skills and broad African experience, and are independent-minded but tolerant towards the UN bureaucracy.

Staffing problems aside, it seems obvious that the MULPOCs are a realistic response to contemporary African needs and political realities. Evidence of this is the list of subjects the council of ministers of the East and Southern African UNDATs felt they should discuss at their second conference: subregional trade, rural reconstruction, industrial development, transport, manpower development, funding of the UNDAT, and economic problems of the not-yet-independent countries of the region. Except for the UNDAT funding concern, this list of subjects is not very different from that found at any regional or subregional meeting held under the auspices of the UN; what made the difference was the underlying assumption that whatever the long-term goal may be--the creation of a common market, for example--the immmediate need is for subregional cooperation in areas where objectives could easily be reached. The council made some unspectacular and practical recommendations: collect and publish subregional trade information, institute direct banking relations by creating reciprocal accounts in each other's currencies, prepare a standard code of conduct vis-a-vis foreign investment, establish freight booking and forwarding agencies. The requests made of the UNDAT were in areas which require experts to lay the groundwork so that national and inter-state development activities will not crumble as they have done in the past.[24] Of course, ECA headquarters, or any one of a number of UN agencies, could undertake these activities. The advantages of a MULPOC, theoretically, are that it can let states participate at a more local level, that it can involve member governments and bilateral and multilateral donors, and that it is flexible enough to draw on both international and local resources.

MULPOCs also appear to be in a unique position with regard to matching up international resources with local needs, since they serve as subregional extensions of the ECA which has access to such resources. The MULPOCs' connection with the ECA should make the ECA responsive to local needs--at least more responsive than the old regional offices, which were frequently more concerned with subregional integration than with providing useful services. Moreover, the MULPOCs, if properly staffed and funded, could meet the continent's need for national and multinational consultancy services. I mentioned earlier that African states spend huge sums to acquire development consultants. The availability of MULPOC staff consultants would cut these costs, and probably provide better service since they would be more familiar with local conditions. One would hope also that the MULPOCs could regularize advisory services in areas that are now handled in an *ad hoc* fashion through bilateral arrangements or other international organizations. And, of course, MULPOCs could facilitate inter-state cooperation within a region. The steps taken at the 1976 Kinshasa meeting of Ministers--revitalizing and extending the system of UNDATs, converting them into MULPOCs, and giving them a new structural relationship to the ECA that in effect integrates them into the ECA work program--all appear to be sensible ones.

Throughout this discussion I have emphasized the MULPOCs' potential to bring technical assistance down to a more local level than was possible from ECA headquarters in Addis Ababa; I have emphasized the flexibility of the MULPOCs, and how this quality makes them promising extension mechanisms for ECA. Now I would like to point out two different kinds of benefits that the MULPOCs may offer Africa.

The first is that MULPOCs can make it possible for African states to get the most use out of their limited amount of skilled manpower. An African agricultural expert can be shared by the states within a MULPOC's region, rather than be shipped off to ECA headquarters.

The second is that MULPOCs are intended to fall at some point under the jurisdiction of the member governments that make up a MULPOC subregion. The intriguing possibility therefore presents itself that MULPOCs may someday be absorbed by African inter-state institutions such as ECOWAS. Within the foreseeable future, however, they will be used primarily to pool limited international and African expertise and skilled manpower capacities under the aegis of the ECA.

The historical evolution from ECA subregional offices--intended to help ECA itself become the core of African regional integration--to MULPOCs--extension offices to provide technical assistance--has been quite swift. It would appear that the

ECA's goal today is less to provide a structure for inter-African community formation than to use its institutional capacities to aid its clients in their own national and inter-state development. If the ECA succeeds someday in fully Africanizing the MULPOCs and in having them be absorbed by their member governments into subregional inter-state institutions then the ECA will no longer be competing with inter-state African organizations in the field of inter-state community formation. The ECA has finally begun to redefine its role.

We should anticipate, however, that as inter-African institutions such ECOWAS become stable, further clarification of the role of the ECA's subregional activities will have to take place since the MULPOCs, rather than being integrated into a subregion's own inter-governmental arrangements might continue to come into competition with them.

## Research and Training Centers

The ECA's work program for the 1970s reflects the lessons it learned in the last decade, as well as new international and African trends. Thus it includes the establishment of permanent regional institutions for manpower training--a move away from *ad hoc* workshops and seminars. For example, the ECA has proposed that an African Center in Applied Research and Training in Social Development be created, a suggestion that takes into account not only the urgent need to develop human resources in general, but also the need for a permanent institution with the expertise to provide particular types of training that are unlikely to be available in each nation on the African continent. Such an institution would avoid the cost and potential inappropriateness of overseas training.

This move away from *ad hoc* workshops and towards permanent training facilities has taken place gradually. During the past decade, the ECA has helped build such facilities: the Regional Center for Training in Aerial Survey (in Ife, Nigeria) and the Center for Surveying and Mapping (Nairobi, Kenya).

In its "Revised Framework of Principles for the Implementation of the New International Economic Order in Africa, 1976-1981-1986" the ECA states that "If...the New International Economic Order is to be actively and effectively pursued, the building of a considerable number of new institutions and the reorientation of many existing ones are likely to be required in such areas as local government, research, finance, marketing and distribution, and public enterprises."[25] Other documents set out the sorts of institution that, in principle, will be included in the ECA's 1977-81 work program[26] The development of the following centers is specifically mentioned: A Center for the Design, Adaptation, and Transfer of Industrial Technology; a Center for Iron and Steel Development; a Center for Consulting Engineers and Management Services; and a Center for the Development of the Petrochemical Industry--to name only a few on the list. (The ECA's desire to develop permanent centers for activities where regional and subregional arrangements are appropriate is apparently shared by the UNDP.)[27]

ECA support of regional research and training centers would make sure that emphasis is placed on this type of development in the future. The expected advantages of such centers are many. First, the ECA s desire to engage in 'action-oriented' activities might be satisfied in part by building such institutions. Second, the centers would involve the ECA further in inter-state activities. Third, they fall within the realm of the ECA's long-standing interest in both institution-building and training. Fourth, the development of a network of subject-specific research and training institutions in areas where African states would like to acquire greater self-sufficiency (but where national institutions are not feasible) is consistent with a New International Economic Order and its accompanying emphasis on self-reliance.

Many of the existing centers focus on scientific and technological matters where African pooling of resources is obviously necessary for economic development. However, the ECA is giving its attention to social matters as well, for example, a African Training and Research Center for Women has been developed in Addis Ababa. The proposed regional Center for Research and Training in Social Development covers a wider area. Until now, the assessment of Africa's social development needs and the training of social workers have taken place largely overseas. A regional institution would provide tailor-made consultancy services and training, and would coordinate national activities in a more economical fashion. We can see in the broader and less tangible social-development context that the building of research and training centers is not meant purely for scientific and technological research, but also for improvement of the society as a whole.

## Conclusion

The preceding sections outline the problem the ECA has faced, and still faces in fulfilling that part of its dual mandate that leads it to describe itself as an African regional organization. Since at the continental level the OAU lays claim to speaking on behalf of African interests, the ECA must in the interests of its own legitimization cooperate with the OAU. Even though the OAU lacks the ECA s resources for economic and social development, it contends that it is the only legitimate continental organization in Africa. The ECA's hopes of serving as the focal point for subregional integration ceased to be realistic long ago; its relatively successful contribution to the establishment of various inter-African institutions can be historically documented, but memories are short and few associate the ECA with the African Development Bank or the ECOWAS, now that these organizations are in operation and have their own staffs, memberships, and programs. In short, the ECA has found it exceedingly difficult to win legitimacy as any kind of African institution in the eyes of its African clients.

Conversion of ECA headquarters into a high-caliber think-tank, combined with the establishment of an outreach network of MULPOCs, would help give focus to ECA activities: it would distinguish the ECA from UN specialized agencies, it would allow the ECA to emphasize inter-African cooperation, and it would reduce African dependency on the international system in vital areas of information and expertise. There is little doubt that African states have vast needs for expertise, feasibility studies, and consultancy services, and that the ECA's activities in this area have been so scattered as to make them invisible to both the international community and its African clients. What the ECA must do is define its role more sharply by limiting its activities and by making its institutional capacity more evident to its clients.

There is every reason to say that the ECA, even with all its problems and inefficiencies, is still the most promising institutional mechanism on the African continent, and is still the best-equipped to facilitate the establishment of the sort of regional arrangements that self-reliance and the New International Economic Order suggest. The experience gained over the years (not to mention the ECA's genuine organizational capacities) could with some administrative and intellectual leadership help the ECA play a significant role in Africa. The burden of reorganizing the ECA, and of giving it a direction, lies naturally with the ECA itself, but also lies with the rest of the UN family--without whose reorganization further efforts on the ECA's part would just be exercises in frustration.

Perhaps equal in importance to development of ECA's institutional capacity and special attention to the development of an outreach structure through MULPOCs is ECA's inter-Africa institution-building role. The ECA can and should continue to help its clients build inter-state institutions. It has acquired considerable skill in drafting and negotiating inter-state arrangements; it need not abandon its consistent advocacy of inter-state integration and cooperation--indeed, the need for the ECA's services in this field may increase in the years to come.

The difficulties arise when one tries to see how the ECA's industrial development division (or any of its substantive divisions) might relate its activities to those of other UN agencies. Transforming the specialized agencies into continental organizations seems unrealistic--as is the ECA's hope that it will some day be able to absorb the activities now handled by the specialized agencies. The ECA's desire to be recognized as an 'action-oriented institution,' which has caused it to engage in industrial development activities in competition with UNIDO and FAO, will probably never be fulfilled. Even African clients who complain that the ECA just writes useless studies are not suggesting that it take on the activities now handled by other UN agencies; when these clients call for "fewer words and more action" they do not necessarily mean, as the ECA seems to think they do, that the ECA should launch projects similar to those of UN specialized agencies and bilateral donors. They only mean that the

ECA should develop an identifiable area of competence.

However, neither UN reorganization nor ECA reform will produce meaningful results for African countries unless the African countries themselves make use of the ECA's expertise in national and regional development, and unless African countries legitimize the ECA by designating it as the regional institution responsible for lobbying for its clients interests in the international development assistance community.

ECA has been hesitant to chose a central emphasis in its work program from among its three categories of activities (member of the international development assistant community; builder of inter-African state institutions; the nucleus for inter-African Development). We have seen that ECA's work to date in each of these three categories has produced both progress and frustration for ECA and for its African client states. The leadership of ECA is no doubt correct in repeatedly urging for more funds, staff and client support. Yet is is also true that ECA's work program has consistently remained diffuse. ECA has been unwilling and/or unable to emphasize one category of work over another, and it has been unable to come to terms with the obstacle presented to it by its dual mandate as a UN and as an African organization. ECA's many contributions to African development and regional cooperation should not be obscured by these ongoing problems. However, ECA's ability to more fully realize its potential as a central voice in African economic development in years to come may well rely in large measure on ECA's own willingness and ability to make some hard choices from amongst its many roles and functions and to develop its future work programs in accordance with those choices.

NOTES

1. Most early ECA documents make this point. In addition Robert Gardiner considered generating and collecting development data one of ECA's most urgent tasks.

2. Author's interview with William Brooker, Head of ECA's Statistical unit, at ECA headquarters in Addis Ababa 3/15/76. Mr. Brooker has been with ECA since 1961.

3. Ibid.,E/CN.14/ECO/INF/34, p. 4.

4. E/CN.14/14/WP 61

5. *Ibid.*, p. 27.

6. *Ibid.*, p 31.

7. *Ibid.*, p 49

8. Author's interviews with Samuel Edokayi, a member of the Manpower Unit, on 3/12/76 in Addis Ababa.

9. E/CN 14/ECO/83.

10. E/CN 14/424 pp. 30-33 *A Venture in Self Reliance* (1958-68) is a document produced by ECA and published by the United Nations in an effort to review and explain ECA operations and intentions of its first ten years of existence It is a particularly useful document insofar as Robert Gardiner's priorities and ideas dominate both the assessment of Africa's needs and ECA s accomplishments and the description of ECA's intended future role.

11. ECA Press Release ECA/1233 19 March 1976.

12 E/CN.14/129.

13. E/CN.14/424/p. 34-35.

14. E/CN 14/STC/21.

15. E/CN.14/STC/A PUR. 1.

16. E/CN.14/FISC/1.

17. E/CN.14/AMA/16.

18. Article II, Draft Agreement Concerning the Establishment of the West African Clearing House.

19. GA Resolution 2563 (XXIV) and ECOSOC Res 1552 (XLIX).

20. "Attack on Absolute Poverty in Africa." New York, ECA, 1974, p. 12.

21. E/CN.14/664, p. 3.

22. *Ibid.*, p. 3-4.

23. *Ibid.*, p. 1-5.

24. ECA Inter-Office Memorandum 11 May 1976, Ref TA 210/1 (119-24) SEA.

25. E/CN.14/90, Rev. 2, p. 16.

26. E/CN.14/ECO/82, p. 3.

27. E/CN.14/ECO/84.

# 5
# Regionalism Reconsidered

## INTRODUCTION

In each international system actors can be expected to be compared to others who perform similar tasks. It has been customary during most of the past two decades to judge ECA with reference to theories of regional integration and to compare ECA to similar and competing United Nations and African institutions. This chapter will begin by following this established practice. ECA's successes and failures will first be compared to that of the Economic Commission for Latin America, the organization generally regarded as the most potent of the UN's Regional Economic Commissions.[1] Next, other UN institutions and the Organization for African Unity will be discussed to ascertain how ECA stands in relationship to other institutions attending to Africa's economic and social development needs.

In the 1970s it has continued to be fashionable to compare and contrast institutions and to judge their respective achievements in fostering inter-state integration and cooperation, but a new element has been added. Contemporary theorists and African client states increasingly have come to challenge ECA and its relevance to African development on the basis of the broader discussion regarding a New International Economic Order (NIEO). The NIEO has at its core the notion that future development of African states resides less in maximizing the work of this or that international or inter-state institution, but assumes instead that all policy activities at the international level need to be directed to a restructuring of the international system as a whole. A new and more equitable distribution of the world's resources is being demanded by actors and advocated by theorists. Indeed a new consciousness exists both amongst LDCs and industrial states to the effect that some kind of international restructuring will have to take place. Because of this discussion, the future of all inter-state organizations concerned with African development is increasingly being judged by new criteria. Since many theorists, ideologues and actors are advocating systemic structural reforms, they tend to measure the ECA on the basis of its ability to help foster a New International Economic Order and its capacity to translate newly acquired resources into meaningful national development. The leadership of ECA has taken cognizance of this new intellectual and political environment and is seeking to respond to it. The future of ECA as a meaningful contributor to African development hinges, in my view, on its ability as an institution to contribute to and respond effectively to this new environment. This chapter will close with a discussion of ECA's response as a UN Commission with a regional perspective to the demands for a New International Economic Order.

## THE ECONOMIC COMMISSION FOR LATIN AMERICA

It is safe to say that of all the Regional Commissions, the ECLA has made the greatest impact to date--if one measures impact in terms of influence on the thinking about regionalism and about the relationship of national and regional development to international economic questions. It is always difficult to trace the pedigree of an idea, but we can trace the evolution of regional efforts in Latin America, such as the Latin American Free Trade Association (LAFTA), the Central American Common Market, and the more recently-formed Andean Commission, to ECLA-generated ideas, work, and support. ECLA developed a distinctive development ideology in the 1960s under the dynamic leadership of its executive secretary, Raul Prebisch. This ideology was further elaborated in the United Nations Conference on Trade and Development (UNCTAD) when Prebisch left ECLA and joined that organization. This ideology is identifiable today as the foundation upon which the NIEO is built.

From its inception, the ECLA had to serve a region which contained considerable political schisms but which, compared with the African continent, enjoyed greater cultural and linguistic uniformity, a longer post-colonial history, and better economic health (measured in GNP). In addition, the Latin American region had a good number of well-trained administrators and technicians who were willing and able to serve in a Regional Commission without creating manpower shortages in their own countries. Instead of developing an elaborate organizational structure, Prebisch concentrated the ECLA's energies in a relatively small (about 100 professionals) secretariat; he gathered the best minds in Latin American economic and social development, and set out to design an economic development ideology.[2] By 1960, the ECLA had become a 'think-tank' for what is today acknowledged, by advocates and critics alike, as an important analysis of underdevelopment.

The essence of the ideology developed by the ECLA was that the economic disadvantages of Third World countries stem from the fact that they are situated in the periphery of an international economic system that has resulted from, and is perpetuated by giving Third World countries unfavorable terms of trade. To attack these disadvantages, industrialized 'core' states would have to be persuaded to reverse this pattern and create in its stead a mechanism that would guarantee preferential status for the LDCs in the periphery.[3] In the context of ECLA ideology, Latin American regional cooperation and integration became an essential step in the reorganization of center-periphery relations--a step that would safeguard against uneven development of states in Latin America.

The development of ECLA ideology required a two-pronged task of the ECLA as a Regional Commission. First, it had to influence international thinking about, and understanding of the nature of underdevelopment, so that the international structure could be altered. In this capacity, the ECLA acted as a lobbyist for Latin America (and for other regions of the Third World as well) within the larger UN structure and within the international system as a whole. The ECLA also served as a think-tank for developing strategies for exerting leverage at the UN and with other multilateral and bilateral agencies. As a result, ECLA ideology became well-known in relevant circles around the world. Not everyone agreed with their analysis, but behind their rhetoric lay a good deal of compelling thought.

The second part of ECLA's task produced an impressive description of, and prescription for, the necessary changes that should take place within Latin American countries and in relations among them. The ECLA did detailed studies on fostering national development and played a key role in establishing regional mechanisms, such as free trade areas and common markets. Since the staff of the ECLA was made up largely of Latin Americans who in many cases later returned to the intellectual and technocratic circles of their own countries, the ECLA's ideas also found their way into some Latin American government ministries. The ECLA has been criticized on the grounds that it neglected diplomatic, political, and institutional tasks, and thus was not always successful in spreading its ideas beyond the limited circle of ECLA supporters; nevertheless, its ideas, if not always carried out, were always exchanged with national ministries and with actors in the international system.

The ECLA was formed as an organization of Latin Americans dedicated to analyzing their own particular underdevelopment problems, and finding strategies to overcome them. Under Prebisch's leadership, and with the availability of high-caliber manpower, a Latin American think-tank was possible.

It should be added that the ECLA suffered no serious organizational competition in the 1950s and '60s. The Organization of American States (OAS) for example was regularly accused by Latin Americans of being dominated by US economic imperialism. It was not difficult, therefore, for the ECLA to acquire prestige as a somewhat radical, anti-international-economic-status-quo organization. In theory, the economic arm of the OAS (the Inter-American Economic and Social Council, or IA ECOSOC) and the ECLA are competitive institutions; but in practice, it is the ECLA who is seen as having taken the initiative in speaking, both inside and outside the region, on behalf of Latin America's interests.

Thus in spite of identifiable failings, and justifiable criticism regarding its actual achievements, the ECLA came to be perceived as a truly Latin American organization, and not as an administrative arm of the United Nations. That is, the ECLA resolved its dual mandate by consciously forfeiting the task of administering UN affairs in Latin America, and serving instead as a brain trust for diagnosing and curing Latin America's ills at the national, continental, and international levels. It neither developed facilities for, nor sought the role of a technical assistance and aid agency for the region; it neither directly facilitated the work of the UN specialized agencies nor competed with them.

As we have seen, the structure and role of the ECA has taken a quite different shape--not merely because the African continent presents different problems for development, but because the ECA came to interpret its dual role in a different way. It should be borne in mind, however, that the import of the ECLA lies not merely in its interpreting, in a different way from the ECA, its role as a Regional Commission, but in its contribution to thinking about the relationship of nation, regional, and international components of economic and social development. The ECLA is the source of a number of ideas that continue to inform the thinking about an NIEO and about the national and regional infrastructure that must accompany international structural changes. The experiences of the ECLA also suggest one way in which a Regional Commission can play a useful role: serving the needs of a region, both inside the region and in the larger international system.

## ECA: A CAUSE WITHOUT A MISSION

Throughout the 1960s, the majority of the professional staff of the ECA, in sharp contrast to that of the ECLA, was not indigenous. Due to the general shortage of technical and administrative experts in Africa, it took the ECA until well into the '70s to Africanize its staff. However, the shortage of indigeneous experts did not keep the staff small; by the mid-'60s, it was bigger than the staffs of both the ECLA and the ECAFE.

Also unlike the ECLA, the ECA did not commence its career with a dominant creative force in development thinking like Raul Prebisch; the ECA's first executive secretary, Mekki Abas, served for a very short time and was succeeded by Robert Gardiner, who in turn spent the first year of his tenure not at the ECA but on assignment in the

Congo. When Gardiner did take full command of his position, he had neither the administrative style nor the intellectual bent to produce a distinctive organizational ideology. Structurally, the ECA did not concentrate its energies in a single secretariat, but developed instead a fairly elaborate system of subregional offices and functional institutions. In addition, the ECA took on the task of administering regional projects for the UN.

By the end of the ECA's first decade (1958-68), it was still groping for a sense of African identity, and was still perceived in Africa (and elsewhere) as a product of the UN, rather than as an African agency. Africanization of the staff was still far from completion, and it had made only moderate inroads on defining Africa's individual and collective needs. In short, the ECA's mission, unlike the ECLA's, was still fuzzy; the tasks it was trying to carry out were more diverse than those of the ECLA. The day that the ECA would be perceived inside and outside Africa as a major authority on describing and prescribing for Africa's development needs was still far in the future.

One explanation for the ECA's failure, after 6 or 8 years of operation, to define its role philosophically and programatically either in Africa or within the UN family, was that the ECA needed to do extensive preparatory work before it could develop an effective program. Robert Gardiner asserted as late as 1966[4] that he spent his initial years at the ECA trying to build a data base upon which a development program could be built in the future. Gardiner defended the organization's information-gathering role as one that served all interested parties--the African states, the UN family, and other bilateral and multilateral donors.

The structure and work routine of the ECA staff reflected its emphasis on generating statistical and other data. Vast numbers of studies were undertaken on industry, transport, manpower; the statistical division began work on a standard for uniform national and UN statistical reporting. The studies themselves reflected the development fashions of the day: in the early and mid-'60s, a good deal more emphasis was placed on industrial than on agricultural development.

Most of the ECA's professional staff had economics or other social science training. This type of staff might have been appropriate if the ECA had, like the ECLA, been considering itself a think-tank for development analysis and strategies; since, however, the ECA was trying to prepare technical background materials, the shortage of technical staff became evident in the general quality of the reports and studies. The ECA's single water or roads expert tended to labor in relative isolation, sometimes directed to undertake a study for which a larger technical staff was absolutely necessary, but frequently guided only by his own interest or inclination.

There was a good deal of validity to the argument that the African continent was so bereft of data, statistics, and other essential information that the ECA was justified in choosing the task it did; Africa's deficiencies in this respect certainly exceeded that of, say, Latin America. It is also true that the ECA in its first ten years produced a large volume of background studies, feasibility studies, and statistical information. The question remains whether the qualify of the ECA's work in amassing background information would not have been better, had it been done within the framework of a well-defined developmental analysis and strategy for Africa. It seemed quite clear to me in 1966 that the ECA's role, as well as its organizational mission lacked focus.[5] As a consequence, much of the ECA's spade work, whatever its technical merit, exhibited a great deal of randomness; furthermore, the ECA staff lacked a sense of organizational ideology, commitment, and direction.

Beyond structural and leadership problems, the ECA also confronted a number of environmental problems: the post-independence Anglophone-Francophone split, for example. The ECA, echoing the UN, opposed the EEC-Francophone relations that were formalized in the Yaounde Agreements.[6] English-speaking African leaders argued that the Yaounde Agreements fostered neo-colonialism and undermined African regional and subregional cooperation. The ECA found itself in the middle of this discussion because its key African staff (including Robert Gardiner, a native of Ghana) was seen as representing only English-speaking Africa's interests. ECA staff members gave implicit and explicit support to the general UN position against EEC-African arrangements, and studies undertaken by the ECA sought to demonstrate the ill-advisedness of EEC-African links.[7] The ECA also protested that French-speaking Africa was not making manpower available to the ECA--which was understandable, given the relatively greater shortage of manpower in French-speaking countries. Not surprisingly, French-speaking Africa regarded the ECA with some negativism throughout the 1960s.

The Anglophone-Francophone schism in Africa did not, of course, affect only the ECA; many African subregional organizations reflected this schism. Nevertheless, the split had serious implications for a Commission intended to serve the continent as a whole. Francophone antagonism toward the ECA was an instance where African arrangements that were based on neo-colonial pressure interfered with African inter-state organization. There is a good deal of evidence that France used the Yaounde Agreements to encourage the African states associated with the EEC to place their development hopes on receiving aid and services from France; since French-speaking African countries were accustomed to such aid, it took little effort to convince themselves that the ECA bore little relation to their interests or needs. French-speaking Africa's tendency, toward the late '60s, to rely on their former colonial ties kept them from participating through staffing or exploitation of ECA development aid, in many of the ECA's activities. In spite of its antagonism, Francophone Africa did not completely abandon interest in the ECA. In 1967 they attempted to oust Robert Gardiner and replace him with a French-speaking African--which suggests at least a minimal amount of interest in the ECA, even if it did take the form of trying to bring it into the French-speaking camp.[8]

By the same token, the relationship of French-speaking Africa to France and the EEC tended to confine interstate relations of French-speaking African countries to sub-groups of former French colonies (UDEAC, OCAM, etc.). This lends some accuracy to the Marxists' accusation that regional integration was a tool of the neo-colonialists--especially when seen from the vantage point of the ECA, which was victimized in its efforts to achieve integration among states where economic logic, rather than neo-colonial ties, should have determined regional arrangements. What I am suggesting here is that in addition to the ECA's English-speaking slant (due to its initial staffing), external forces also tended to undermine the support and participation of French-speaking Africa in the identification of the ECA as an effective actor in African development affairs.

## THE OAU VERSUS THE ECA

The establishment of the Organization of African Unity (OAU) in 1963 also affected the ECA's role and mission.[9] The relationship between the OAU and the ECA, both of whom have headquarters in Addis Ababa, has always been complex, and reflects each of the organization's strengths and weaknesses.

It is important to recall that the ECA had already been in existence for five years when the OAU's Economic and Social Commission first met in Naimey, Niger, in December, 1963. The OAU from its very inception lacked the staff and resources with which to contribute to African regional economic and social development; just the same, its first secretary-general, Francophone Diallo Telli, spent a lot of time pointing out that the ECA, as a UN organ, was unsuited to handle a number of economic and social issues--especially those where African political questions were involved. As I have mentioned earlier, the assigned functions and structure of the OAU were decided upon as a compromise between the more radical Casablanca and the more moderate Monrovia groups; nevertheless, the tone established by the OAU and fostered by Telli, was one of a Pan-Africanist organization firmly opposed to neo-colonialism. It presented itself as the one organization that could unite all those disparate African voices calling for an African bloc to represent African interests in international forums.

The ECA, just down the road, paled in comparison both politically and ideologically; since the ECA had not yet succeeded in establishing itself, either as an all-African institution or as a lobbyist for African interests in the international community, it was relatively easy for the OAU to win more popularity. All it had to do was point out that the ECA was, in any event, a UN (as opposed to an African) organization, that its staff was dominated by expatriates, and that the few Africans that were on the staff were mostly Anglophones. To make matters worse, the head and several staff members of the ECA were Ghanaians who had a falling-out with Kwame Nkrumah (then still a powerful force in African Unity). In short, the OAU quickly established itself as the organization that spoke politically for and about Africans.

It might be of some interest to recall that, in contrast to the ECA, the ECLA managed to gain widespread Latin American support and, equally importantly, managed to establish itself as the principal lobbyist for Latin American interests--as opposed to the OAS, which was seen as American-controlled and neo-colonial. Thus, the ECLA played the role of a voice for Latin America in spite of its being a UN Regional Commission, while the ECA was tainted by being an arm of the UN in which non-Africans were influential. The birth of the OAU at a time when the ECA still had a fuzzy image, both inside and outside Africa, allowed the OAU to establish its position as the dominant political mechanism on the continent.

Because the ECA's role *vis-à-vis* its African membership was still uncertain, Robert Gardiner recognized that the ECA and the OAU needed to develop some kind of working relationship. The ECA approached the OAU on the matter, although quite cautiously. Both organizations could not help but realize that although the OAU was in a position to exercise political leverage and (rhetorically, at least) register African demands in international forums, it lacked funds and a staff. The ECA's professional staff (almost 100 by the mid-'60s) and its access to the UN's financial and manpower reservoirs made it a potentially very potent force, compared to the OAU's handful of staff members--devoted to economic and social matters--and its almost total lack of funds. The OAU's economic and social development budget relied on the contributions that came through its Scientific and Technical Research Commission (STRC), which had independent headquarters in Lagos, Nigeria, and which possessed a network of regional technical and research groups (inherited by the OAU from the colonially-established CCTA). However, even the facilities and capabilities of the STRC, still largely funded by the metropoles, were miniscule when compared with ECA operations.[10]

By 1965, formal proposals for cooperation between the OAU and the ECA had been made. As a consequence of Diallo Telli's visit to UN headquarters in New York in November, 1965, an agreement was signed that allowed for reciprocal representation at ECA and OAU meetings on economic and social matters.[11]

In practice, the cooperation between the two organizations has had mixed results. A number of meetings, conferences, and seminars, as well as several studies and proposals, carry joint OAU/ECA sponsorship. In almost all cases the actual work on these has been done under the direction of the ECA, while OAU participation has been limited to a legitimizing function; on the African continent, the ECA's image is still so unclear that OAU co-sponsorship is often useful. In international circles, however, any enterprise gains by having ECA sponsorship, since the OAU is often regarded as a somewhat radical, irresponsible, anti-Western organization; the ECA profits in this case from its moderate image and UN affiliation.

It could be argued that the somewhat uncomfortable co-existence of the OAU and the ECA has reinforced the weaknesses of each in economic and social affairs. In spite of almost annual commitments by the OAU to develop its own economic and social programs, potential donors, considering the presence of the relatively well-staffed and funded ECA, tend to drag their feet. Similarly, the OAU's claims to speak in a collective African voice have probably served as an obstacle, at least in the past, to ECA efforts to give itself a more politicized image at home and abroad. It is my conclusion, therefore, that ECA/OAU co-existence has strengthened neither organization, but rather has aggravated the disabilities of each.

There is one area in which the existence of the OAU may have been of help to the ECA. Because OAU meetings serve as the rhetorical platforms on which African states give their views on such issues as racism, colonialism, neocolonialism, and capitalism, ECA meetings are left with relatively low-keyed rhetoric and more focused discussions of economic development policies. That is, the existence of the OAU serves to depoliticize ECA meetings. The argument can be made that the OAU, by providing an arena for conflicts between African states and between Africa and the international environment, enables the ECA to carry on its annual policy and planning meetings in a relatively businesslike atmosphere. (In this respect ECA's meetings compare favorably with those of the ECAFE which, in the absence of an equivalent of the OAU, include speechifying similar to that of the OAU--which goes on for a number of days before any serious work on economic development policy can be done.)

It can also be argued, of course, that the OAU's deflecting the political spotlight is not completely to the advantage of the ECA; the ECA might be invigorated by greater, and higher level political concern on the part of its member states. Whatever the merit of such a suggestion, the inability of OAU delegates to unite on many important political issues (not counting the issues that simply get stalemated) suggests that inter-African schisms in the 1970s are so deep that the ECA would hardly gain from becoming the battleground for political conflicts that are only of indirect interest to an organization concerned with economic and social development.

Seen from a historical perspective the ECA, prior to the creation of the OAU in 1963, clearly failed to develop the sense of mission and the image that might have given it the sort of potency the ECLA achieved in Latin America. As a consequence it was the OAU that, in spite of the ECA's seniority as an organization, quickly capitalized on the need for an organization dedicated to politicizing African views and demands. The ECA, due to African circumstances (and some conscious choices on Robert Gardiner's part), sought to resolve its dual mandate not by selecting one emphasis, but rather by trying to operate both as an arm of the UN and as an organization dedicated to serve its clients. Unlike the ECLA, the ECA came to be perceived as just one more UN agency.

## THE ECA AND THE UN SYSTEM

We will recall that the ECLA avoided becoming an arm of the UN economic and social development machinery. It did not on the whole participate in UNDP or in Specialized Agency projects, nor did it develop technical assistance facilities that duplicated or competed with sectorial specialties of UN agencies. The ECA, on the other hand, tried to develop facilities that would allow it to become both the project-generating and project-implementing arms of the UN system on the African continent. This goal posed two problems for the ECA. First, its institutional capacities were inadequate to these tasks; a handful of experts in, say, agriculture, were hardly in a position to compete with the FAO in project development and/or execution. Second, African states became accustomed, early after independence, to dealing with UN Specialized Agencies either through their regional headquarters in Africa or at agency headquarters overseas; that is, they become habituated to circumventing the ECA when seeking development aid from the UN system. Because it did not develop a specific set of functions or sense of mission, the ECA gave the impression that it was not the UN agency to approach with a specific development request.

While African countries continued to deal with UN Specialized Agencies throughout the 1960s, the ECA tried to establish some relationship with the agencies in order to avoid duplication of effort and to find a way of using the vast resources of the Specialized Agencies to supplement the limited ones of the ECA. By the end of the 60s even some Specialized Agencies were concerned with identifying the structural relationship and activities of Specialized Agencies in Africa with those of an all-purpose Regional Commission. In 1968, for example, FAO Director-General, A.H. Boerma, suggested moving the FAO's regional office for Africa from Accra, Ghana, to ECA headquarters in Addis Ababa.[12] This might have given the ECA a clearly-defined identity as the regional operational arm of UN Specialized Agencies--a role different from that which the ECLA played in Latin America but a promising first step in clarifying the ECA's mission, nonetheless.

However, this potentially constructive move was never made, for a variety of reasons; UN Specialized Agency regional offices opposed the idea, as did countries playing host to the regional offices (e.g., Ghana and the FAO), who did not want to lose the prestige of having UN bureaus in their midsts. What was perhaps more serious and more damning was that a number of African states opposed such a role for the ECA. Francophone countries were opposed as a group, and so were the other African countries who had more faith in UN Specialized Agencies than in the ECA.[13] This turn of events demonstrated the degree to which (after ten years in operation and the accumulation of the largest professional staff of any UN regional organization) the ECA failed to define its mission either in terms of its work or its environment.

In spite of the Africanization of its staff,[14] some joint ECA Specialized Agency activities, calls for emphasis on 'action programs' instead of background studies, increased availability of bilaterial funds, and the perennial claims of the OAU that it would expand its own efforts in the economic and social realm, the ECA was still suffering from its split personality in 1975 when Robert Gardiner was succeeded by the Nigerian Adebayo Adedeji.

In retrospect, we can see that the ECA, unlike the ECLA, emphasized the part of its mandate that assigned it duties as an operational arm of the UN's economic and social development structure. However, the ECA continued to grope within the UN maze, duplicating the work of some Specialized Agencies, competing with others, and seeking to coordinate its activities, while many of its clients grew more uncertain about what the ECA's capacities might be. Rather than resolving its mandate in favor of becoming an African organization (as the ECLA had become a Latin American organization), the ECA instead emphasized its structural relationship to the UN system--without clarifying its own distinctive role within that system, or achieving legitimacy and support from its African clientele.

## CONCLUSION

What has been at issue in this discussion is not that the ECA failed to duplicate the ECLA's role and success, but that the ECA failed to develop any identifiable profile at all. While its leadership and staff should be partially held to account for this, it should also be borne in mind that the ECA merely reflected many of Africa's deficiencies: political and cultural schisms, a large number of states, an absence of regional and national infrastructures, a shortage of manpower at national and regional levels, and a psychological disposition in favor of visibly quick economic development and against incremental changes. ECLA called for radical changes in the international economic structure and offered Latin American countries blueprints for national and regional development. The ECA, on the other hand, offered members statistical tables, feasibility studies, and charters for regional arrangements--leaving it to members to individually or collectively call for international restructuring. It can be suggested that the ECLA offered its membership an ideology with which to generate increased resources internationally, and to maximize their use regionally. The ECA during its first 20 years did not offer its membership an ideology that would help generate external resources, though it did suggest that regional arrangements could make the best use of continental resources; it took as its primary task increased national and regional capacities in the areas of statistics, data collection, feasibility studies, manpower training, and institution building--lacks of which were (and continue to be) major obstacles to African development.

The accuracy of Robert Gardiner's estimates regarding African needs are not in doubt; but the ECA's role in meeting those needs does call for close scrutiny. Raul Prebisch seems to have sensed the importance of leadership and creative thought in addressing development issues, but Gardiner's bureaucratic and diplomatic inclinations, normally welcome in international organizations, may have been helpful only insofar as they reflected the balkanization of the continent--they certainly did not help to overcome it. The ECLA sought to change Latin American and international consciousness. The fact that the ECA became a main proponent of regional integration in Africa, important as it has been, should nevertheless be seen in its historical context: as reflecting less on African political and economic realities and more on international thinking of the 1960s, which was based on European experience and Latin American efforts. The ECA did not develop new thinking about regional integration or about the causes of underdevelopment. But the very fact that it <u>did</u> advocate, and lay the groundwork for regional arrangements had important consequences (as we have seen in Chapter 4) for the future of regional capacities in Africa.

## THE NEW INTERNATIONAL ECONOMIC ORDER: A NEW FACTOR ENTERS THE DISCUSSION

The Economic Commission for Africa, as other UN Regional Commissions, evolved during a period of history when theorists and ideologues advocated regional and subregional institution building. In Africa the ECA in turn not only contributed to regional institution building but itself became a missionary for the ideas contained in regional integration and cooperation, and at the same time helped to shape the African institutions which made up the status quo. However as the 1960s came to a close, new interpretations and demands were offered to diagnose the obstacles to economic development and to advocate solutions to them. Ideas once thought to be the preserve of Latin Americans and radical critics began to move into the mainstream of discussion earlier taken up by regional integration and cooperation advocates.

In the 1970s theorists and LDCs have come to argue, individually and collectively, that national growth and development are contingent on fundamental changes in the international economic system. Closing, or even narrowing the poverty gap is said to be dependent on permanent structural changes in matters such as terms of trade, access to markets, international monetary reforms, and protection of purchasing power--to name only the most salient areas. The stop-gap resource-and-skill transfers of the past 20 years, they say, did not achieve in the past (and cannot be expected to achieve in the future) the global redistribution necessary to closing the poverty gap. The phrase New International Economic Order has become the slogan for those among both poor and rich states who agree that global economic restructuring is an essential step to narrowing the gap between LDCs and affluent industrial countries.[15]

International economic restructuring is represented by its advocates as the best strategy for achieving national economic growth and development. Within the past few years the NIEO has become the centerpiece of development thinking for many international agencies and forums, ranging from the United Nations and its family of agencies to the Trilateral Commission. Restructuring the international economic order has been the main agenda item in the so-called North-South dialogue of the mid-1970s.

Confrontations regarding the NIEO have been carried on within the context of most United Nations-sponsored meetings, such as the 1976 UNCTAD in Nairobi, Kenya. In addition, a special forum for the North-South dialogue, the Conference on International Cooperation, met in Paris in 1976 and 1977.[16] At issue throughout the North-South discussions have been questions regarding the magnitude of resource transfers between the North and South, the establishment of international mechanisms to assure stabilization of commodity prices, and access to technology. Both sides in the dialogue appear to accept the necessity for change but opinions differ as to the magnitude and the implementation of changes.

At the conclusion of the Paris Conference, this much became clear: the industrial countries are still unwilling to meet the demands of the LDCs, but they have managed to camouflage this unwillingness so successfully--by speaking reasonably and appearing to accept the need for an NIEO--that the LDCs' rhetorical advantage has been decreased. The LDCs further weakened their own position by making some tactical errors and by failing to come to a unified stand on a number of issues. Once one moves away from the general principles of the NIEO and begins to discuss what its specific components ought to be, different priorities and plans come to separate the LDCs from one another--divisions exist between industrial states in their willingness to transfer resources and to support major structural reforms.[17]

The LDCs managed to gain leverage at various mid-70s conferences concerned with these North-South issues precisely because they had been able to achieve a remarkable degree of cohesiveness; it was this cohesiveness that literally forced the industrial states to enter into the North-South dialogue. One can see that, given great diversity among the LDCs, unity would be difficult to maintain once discussions passed beyond rhetorical demands and into specific proposals for economic restructuring. Some proposals would benefit only the better-off LDCs; others would benefit only certain regions. The difficulty of keeping a unified position became evident at the Paris dialogue when inter-LDC conflicts weakened the bargaining position of the South.

In contrast, the industrial states have been placed on the defensive by the collective Third World demands for international restructuring which, in the eyes of the industrial states, lump too many complex economic issues into an unmanageable package. While they have given in to the general demand that they work towards an NIEO, industrial states have sought to disaggregate demands by dealing with LDCs bilaterally rather than as a bloc. The US believes, for example, that debt moratoria ought to be worked out on a case-by-case basis, rather than on the across-the-board basis the LDCs demanded. Industrial states have indicated a preference for working on raw material price stabilization on a case-by-case basis, rather than adopting a set of guidelines covering all raw materials. The collective bargaining approach--demands for international economic reforms and for across-the-board treatment of the issues--clearly suits the needs of the LDCs: cohesiveness strengthens the bargaining position of individually weak states. On the other hand, a state-by-state, issue-by-issue approach allows the industrial states to dictate the extent to which changes in the international economic system will take place. At this writing, it is difficult to say whether schisms between LDCs will continue to make possible bilateral responses to their demands, or whether GATT, UNCTAD and IMF conferences in the months to come will reinvigorate collective LDC efforts.

What is clear is that while demands for the NIEO have not brought about concrete structural changes in the international system, they have reflected the increased bargaining power of the LDCs. The question now is whether an international structure can be built that will allow the LDCs to further increase this bargaining power--increase it until it can gain the kind of genuine structural changes that will foster development and narrow the North-South poverty gap.

Underlying the NIEO is the belief that neither pump-priming economic aid, nor regional integration as advocated and advanced in the 1950s and 1960s, can overcome the international structural conditions that produced the disparity that now exists between the North and the South. It is assumed that global restructuring will guarantee an ongoing transfer of resources, and safeguard against the endemic disadvantage from which the LDCs have suffered in the international economy.

There is no disputing the fact that the old international economic order has not worked to the advantage of African states; the injustices and disparities of the old order, and the adverse consequences that have afflicted African states, need not be recited. Neither will it be disputed here that an NIEO is a desirable goal for the international community as a whole. What is at issue is whether or not changes envisioned by the NIEO will in and of themselves make a marked impact on the economic life of most African states. Care must be taken that the NIEO does not in the final analysis remain a promising set of theories (the way those of economic aid and regional integration did) that leaves African countries and their peoples further behind economically.

One of the most crucial flaws in much of the theorizing about, and advocacy for, African development in past decades has been its emphasis on development through the transfer of capital resources. As one African observer recently pointed out, the tragedy for Africa is that it came into the stream of things just when the transfer of capital seemed the solution to all problems. But for Africa it is not the transfer of capital, but the capacity to generate the skills, managerial know-how, administrative capacity, and psychological outlook that will allow development to take place.[18] Economic aid in the 1950s and 1960s failed to face these needs. Regional cooperation and integration efforts assumed that African states needed (in addition to capital transfers) to pool their resources to achieve economic development; but they did not take into adequate account the fact that if a country lacks managerial and administrative know-how, national incapacities are simply transferred into the regional realm. Regional integration theories, which led to the proliferation of inter-African organizations, assumed that pooling of minimal capacities would be beneficial when in fact the capacities did not exist at all, or were so minimal that there was little to pool. Advocates of regionalism also tended to assume that regional groupings would maximize externally-generated capital resources, but given the minimal institutional infrastructure of most African regional arrangements, and given donor preferences for bilateral investments, most capital transfers from industrial countries to African states circumvented the existing regional mechanisms.[19]

Two solutions to Africa's problems have been put forward in the mid-seventies. The first states that we must recognize that Africa's economic situation is in part the consequence of a global economic structure which, if reformed, would allow Africa to move into a more advantageous and competitive international economic position. The second contends that the transfer of resources made through the NIEO should be used to achieve greater national self-reliance, so that the economy and policy of each state can be self-determined and developed.

There are some dangers, however, in discarding the formulas and theories of the past few decades in favor of the NIEO and hopes for greater national self-reliance. In advocating necessary structural changes in the international system, the NIEO tends, like the development strategies of the past, to concentrate on generating capital resources. Thus in the 1970s, as in the 1960s, inadequate attention is given to generating African capacities in managerial and administrative skills, without which additional capital resources may once again fail to achieve development.

Given the characteristics of the African continent, it may well be that national development and self-reliance can only be achieved by an NIEO _if_ there is a concurrent emphasis on workable African regional arrangements. Given the African context, it is worth asking whether national development is even possible (within the context of the NIEO) _without_ some regional pooling. Clearly there are some tasks that are best tackled on a world-wide basis, tasks in which the effective operational decisions are not within the power of any one country or any group of countries: international monetary reform obviously requires world-wide attention. There are also activities that are best handled on local levels, such as integrated rural development.

However, there is a wide range of activities connected with recruitment, negotiation, and resource mobilization which groups of countries with common interests might do through regional or subregional organizations. It is easier in the 1970s than it was in the '60s for groups of African countries to identify realistic common goals. An important element in the successful working of contemporary regional arrangements is that a particular group of countries has concrete reasons to establish an inter-governmental mechanism. The membership in many post-colonial regional arrangements was based less on concrete needs and reasonable expectations than it was on previous colonial relations and utopian visions of integrated communities. Today there is far more reason to establish intergovernmental agencies among countries whose ideologies, economies, or geographic locations have already led to interstate relations. For instance, a currency clearing house makes sense now that currency interaction makes it convenient; it did not make sense 15 or 20 years ago when there were few such transactions. In short, the time is now ripe--which is was *not* in the '60s--for African states to make arrangements that facilitate their interaction and allow them to maximize the utility of limited resources. In addition, regional and subregional groups will make it possible for African states to organize and to exert leverage on their own behalf in the international realm. In this latter sense, African regionalism allows for collective self-reliance in international negotiations where individual self-reliance given the size and potency of many African states, would not be effective.

In the years to come, many of the more than 75 existing African intergovernmental organizations will continue to be inoperative; a few will flourish. Perhaps some new ones will be formed. What is important to recognize is that failures of regionalism in the past were part of the total failure to understand the real obstacles to African development. The realization on the part of African states that self-reliance is an important component of the NIEO is only part of the answer. In addition, there should be a reassessment of the need for, and the functions of, existing and yet-to-be-created regional mechanisms.

It was erroneous to assume that capital resource transfers, some technical assistance, and the superimposition of regional mechanisms could break the back of poverty in Africa. It would be equally erroneous to assume that better terms of trade, greater availability of capital resources, and more national self-reliance can quickly overcome poverty. Regional and subregional mechanisms need to be created to help African states overcome skilled-manpower shortages, information and technology gaps, and administrative incapacities at all levels. This will take time, but a number of regional organizations such as ECOWAS, the Mano River Union, the African Development Bank, and the United Nations Regional Commission for Africa are promising developments. In addition, collective action in managing Africa's affairs in the international system would help meet Africa's external development needs.

I do not want to appear to deny the importance of greater sensitivity to the need for systemic changes or to the fact that many issues facing mankind, including economic development, transcend state and regional boundaries. Indeed, I might argue that the recognition of a need for a New International Economic Order is sadly belated. I do want to assert, however, that a New International Order is a necessary, but not sufficient condition for overcoming the obstacles to growth and development facing most LDCs. When regional theories of the 1950s and '60s tried to address the economic-development problems of the LDCs, they usually failed to do so because the theories were based on faulty knowledge of the countries involved; I fear that the development theories based on the NIEO will fail for much the same reasons. The past infatuation with regional integration and the current infatuation with the NIEO have caused similar oversights in attempts to address the development needs of the LDCs--especially of those on the African continent. Too little attention is being paid to the relationship between economic, manpower, and institutional development, and too much emphasis is still being placed on the importance of capital resource transfers and better terms of trade. In fact, this swing from advocacy of regional integration to that of an NIEO seems to obscure some of the major obstacles that obstructed regional integration (in both its theoretical and concrete manifestations) in the first place.

It is within this context that I have argued, in this study, that regionalism (as distinct from regional integration) continues to be a relevant force, and that Africa's experience with regionalism has had more success than many people give it credit for in laying the groundwork for development. I have also argued that regional cooperation in Africa will have to increase in the years to come if an NIEO is to have the effect of improving the rate of economic development in most African states. My advocacy of regionalism is instrumental--that is, I include everything from loose regional cooperation to regional integration, provided it facilitates development. My underlying interest is not in inter-state community formation--the end goal of regional integration theory--but rather the economic development that would provide an improved standard of living for those on the margins of survival in Africa.

For Africa, a key obstacle to development during the past decades has been an inadequate institutional and manpower capacity with which to translate capital into meaningful development. Equally important has been Africa's lack of institutional and manpower capacity with which to generate and then maximize new resources for development. In spite of many failures in the area of inter-state community-building, the track record of African inter-state institution building and cooperation has improved considerably over the past decade. Indeed, some of the preconditions for regional integration that did not exist in the 1950s and '60s--inter-state trade, communication links, and policy-coordination capabilities--are now present. I am not predicting the imminent arrival of regional integration in Africa. I am saying that a fair amount of regional cooperation and regional institution-building has in fact taken place and can be expected to increase in the years to come. The importance of this process strikes me as central if greater national self-reliance is to become a reality for African states individually and collectively within the context of the realization of a more just international economic order. Perhaps more importantly, ECA's spade work and future potential can contribute to developing the proper role for African regional activity in the context of discussions of NIEO and greater self-reliance.

## ECA'S RESPONSE AND POTENTIAL ROLE IN THE NIEO

Focusing our discussion on the ECA has allowed us to see more clearly both the policies for and obstacles to economic development through regional integration and cooperation. The ECA's dual mandate--its duties both as an arm of the international development assistance community and as an African regional organization--have placed it at the intersection of national, regional and international development efforts. The ECA's policies and programs reflect prevalent development strategies; its areas of effectiveness reflect not only its own institutional weaknesses but African obstacles to development strategies as well. In the past few years the ECA too has begun to take note of the shift in popularity away from regional integration and towards the NIEO, and has sought to adjust its own outlook and strategies accordingly. Specifically, the ECA has taken the initiative on addressing the question of its own role in an NIEO. It has produced a document--"Revised Principles for Implementation of the New International Economic Order in Africa, 1976-1981-1986"[20] (referred to as ECO 90)--that aims and in many ways succeeds in translating the rhetoric of the NIEO into a program of examining the regional and sub-regional dimensions of the NIEO issues. The Document also suggests what the ECA's contribution might be.

ECO 90 takes into account the subsistence nature of most African economies, and the fragmented national markets for industrial products; it suggests that under these circumstances inter-state cooperation is essential to socio-economic change on the continent.[21] The introduction to the document lists the obstacles to inter-African cooperation as 1) conceptual inadequacies; 2) institutional deficiencies; and 3) insufficient attention to instrumentation.[22] It goes on to point out that the conditions in, and therefore the proper solutions for developing African countries are different in many salient respects from those in other countries. The condition in African states, it reports, are characterized by "an inadequate supply of competent entrepreneurs in both the public and private sectors; a scarcity of skilled manpower; limited familiarity with the sources of raw material supply, the range of choice of technology, production processes, and product markets; limited inter-industry integration; large imports of products; small output mix (including poor utilization of by-products); and limited domestic markets relative to plant sizes."[23] The document goes on to argue that close cooperation among member-states is more likely to secure the desired objectives than is individual action. The introduction sagely concludes that while the NIEO is to be supported in its calls for global redistribution (including the flow of external resources into Africa), the realization of African objectives will depend "to a considerable extent on the supply and quality of entrepreneurship and management, conceived in the broadest sense, in both the public and private sectors in Africa."[24] In short, the ECA is calling attention to the work Africa must do before it can reap any benefits from restructuring of the international economic system.

The thoughts expressed in ECO 90 are neither original nor revolutionary. Yet to a student who has paid attention to thought, especially in Africa, on these matters for a decade they suggest a sobriety and maturity that is quite distinct from earlier, more exuberant expectations that regional integration and massive external aid would provide the key to African development.

The report is also sober about, and by implication critical of, the ECA's own policies and programs of the past quarter-century. It admits that individual African governments, in an attempt to apply international theories on development and accelerated economic growth, frequently reinforced the same economic patterns and internal structural inadequacies that the states had had as colonies. When African states recognized increasing instability in export volumes and prices, many of them expanded production and exports in an effort to compensate for falling prices. They also heeded the international call for diversifying the production of agricultural export commodities; but the move away from single-export crops (coffee, cocoa, sisal), rather than leading to increased export earnings for African states, led to a greater number of agricultural export surpluses on the consumer markets of industrial countries. The net effect was to depress the prices of many African export commodities.[25] In short, the ECA often offered its clients conventional international wisdom (based, of course, on the experiences of the industrial states) rather than solutions designed with the structural weaknesses of African states in mind.

It seems fair to suggest, as ECO 90 does, that since the energies of African governments and the ECA were fully taken up with the application of these externally-generated ideas for improving African economies, insufficient attention was paid to the limitations of the inherited structure of national economies, the vacuum in the area of proper statistical information, the lack of knowledge about natural resources bases, the range and quality of research capabilities, the nature and functioning of internal markets, the characteristics and distribution of populations, the internal impact of imported technology and manpower, and the lack of development of indigenous technology and manpower. Social factors in each state were largely ignored. In short, the past two decades in Africa might be characterized by an almost total preoccupation with externally-induced problems and inherited socio-economic institutions.[26] Relatively large investments were made in attempts to foster infrastructural, educational and rural development, but these investments had relatively little yield--a sobering thought for the ECA, since its own identity has been based for the past 15 years on establishing programs and obtaining funding for just such development. The difficulty was that the constraints mentioned earlier--inadequate supply of skilled manpower, extensive dependence on external production and distribution, poor knowledge of domestic resources, externally-oriented transport and communications, dependence on foreign capital, mounting debts, inappropriate application of technology and slow development of appropriate technology--made many investments in regional integration or national development a waste of money.[27]

By the mid-'70s, most African states--and, as this ECA report indicates, some international organizations--have come to the realization that past efforts were simply misdirected. No one had come to terms with the depth and nature of the problems which, combined with the international structural factors, formed the major impediments to development. At the international level one now mainly hears calls for global restructuring and for a stop to the kind of exploitation that helps to perpetuate African under-development. In Africa and in the ECA, however, there is a feeling that the NIEO will only be successful if social and economic problems in Africa are dealt with at the national and regional levels, and that structural limitations in Africa call for greater attention to inter-African relations and cooperation.

ECO 90 is quick to warn against the risk of merely renewing efforts to build inter-African institutions. In a passage that is, once again, indirectly critical of the ECA's own experience in the past two decades it states that "it is not often recognized that the level of competence and efficiency of the machinery at the multinational level depends on the level of competence and efficiency of the machinery at the national level and vice versa."[29] Thus, the report echoes the general dissatisfaction with Africa's national and regional performance to date, and concludes that more of the same approaches will not lead to fundamental improvement, even if and when additional funds for development are made available through redistribution of the world's resources.

This sober, self-critical assessment leads one to anticipate a new set of ideas based not only on having learned from the past but from having found new bearings. But there, sadly, ECO 90 (and indeed, most writings that have emerged from the UN system so far) gives little guidance. Admittedly, it gives a list of priorities: more emphasis on agriculture and integrated rural development, and so on. At this point, however, one expects a little more than a somewhat revised catalogue of problem areas; apparently the ECA has still not discovered the needed creative thought in its midst and harnessed it, nor has it attracted it to Addis Ababa. Indeed, the most hesitant efforts to innovate, to try out new ideas, are lost somewhere in the bureaucratic backwaters that engulf everyone within the UN system.

At this point in our discussion we should address two specific issues. First, how far should we argue that some forms of regionalism are essential components of greater national self-reliance and of a new international economic order? And second, if we argue that regionalism *is* essential to African development in the decades to come, what role, if any, should the ECA play? I believe it would be useful to address first the question of what role the ECA can and ought to play, and then proceed to the larger question of the role and function of regionalism: since the ECA is still the major promoter of regionalism on the African continent, and since its organizational resources are often needed to initiate and sustain regional efforts, the future of regionalism on the African continent and the role and capacity of the ECA are related.

This study has sought to show that despite many shortcomings, the accomplishments of the ECA are important. The organization's attempts to fulfill both parts of its dual mandate, its inability to clarify its mission, its attempts to come up with development strategies and then carry out projects and programs based on those strategies, and its inability to develop bureaucratic efficiency and a high-quality staff, have all combined to give the ECA a mixed reputation among its clients--and have led to bureaucratic malaise at the ECA itself. However, both staff and clients tend to emphasize current problems and to underemphasize needs which have already been met, or are in the process of being met by the ECA. After observing the ECA for two decades, I find its accomplishments to be respectable. The ECA's experience in fostering inter-state institutions and activities is second to none on the African continent. During the better part of its existence the ECA's concern with regionalism was a reflection of mainstream development thinking, but criticism of the ECA was based not on the aims of its policies--not on the thrust of its regional integration and cooperation ideas--but rather on its inability to satisfy client needs. Today, however, the ECA is being called upon not only to demonstrate its ability to produce high-quality studies and programs, but also to justify its advocacy of regionalism in a world where the NIEO and national self-reliance have captured the fancy of many actors and observers. It should come as no surprise, then, that the ECA is seeking to find a place for regionalism within the context of NIEO, and to thereby justify its role and functions in accordance with current fashions in development thinking.

It is interesting to note that during the ECA's first decade, when Robert Gardiner tried to sell regional integration to his clients, the main obstacles were posed by the clients, who were frequently less convinced than the development theorists that regional integration had much to offer--and who were more quickly disappointed when incremental regional integration efforts did not enhance national development. However, the ECA had considerable international support for its efforts in fostering regional integration. Today the ECA's devotion to regionalism must be proved relevant within the context of the now-fashionable NIEO and greater national self-reliance--and yet today the ECA's clients appear to be more inclined to consider the virtues of regional cooperation and regional institution-building. This is so partly because African states have found collective action necessary for negotiating with the larger international community and for facilitating external investment in Africa, but these are not the only reasons for increased African interest in regionalism. Many African states have begun to see that collective action is also a pragmatic means to overcome their national development disabilities. Neither ECOWAS, nor the Mano River Union, nor efforts to build transcontinental roads, can be seen merely as attempts to exert leverage in negotiations or to encourage foreign investment. It seems ironic that at a time when in the world of ideas regionalism is on the decline, in the world of government action and policy in Africa, regionalism has just moved beyond the level of rhetoric.

The ECA is therefore in the position of having to internationally spread propaganda about the relevance of regionalism while feeling, for the first time, that it can take somewhat for granted its clients' willingness to engage in inter-state development. Of course, this ironic turn of events also places new burdens on the ECA and reveals new weaknesses to its clients. What is at issue in _Africa_ today is not whether the ECA's notion of _regional_ cooperation is relevant, but whether the ECA has the capacity to help its clients. The relevance of the ECA as an institution on the African continent is contingent on its ability to efficiently meet client needs in areas not covered by other agencies of the UN, by the OAU, or by bilateral donors.

I think it is clear, from what I have said in Chapter 4, that I think the ECA should give up all or most of its activities under Category I. That category, we will recall, includes all those activities in which the ECA renders _ad hoc_ development assistance--often in areas in which it competes or overlaps with UN Specialized Agencies of with bilateral aid agencies. The ECA has already abandoned most of its Category III activities--those where the ECA, as an institution, tried to make its field offices serve as the nuclei for sub-regional integration. However, the ECA has continued, through the creation of the MULPOCs and the Regional Research and Training Centers, to try to develop a subsidiary institutional structure--thus bringing it into potential competition with some of the institutions it is encouraging its clients to form for themselves. For example: the Economic Commission for Africa and the Economic Community of West African States were recently reported as having signed a cooperation memorandum aimed at promoting multinational economic cooperation in the West African sub-region.[29] On the one hand such an agreement is consistent with ECA efforts to help establish ECOWAS, and merely means that the ECA is committing itself to do the background studies that the ECOWAS will require in order to develop its oprations; or, to put it another way, the ECA is merely planning to give technical assistance to a sub-regional mechanism. But on the other hand, one might ask what the relationship between the ECOWAS and the West African MULPOC is or ought to be. Documents concerning the establishment of the MULPOCs suggest that the centers' activities are intended to be taken over by the sub-region as soon as that becomes feasible. If this is the case, should the ECOWAS someday absorb the West African MULPOC? Or will each institution develop along parallel, and to some extent competitive, lines? These questions call for the immediate attention of the ECA and the existing inter-state organizations, especially if the ECA is to be successful in clarifying its role and functions with respect to the other UN agencies and to the other regional and sub-regional institutions in Africa.

The central focus for ECA reform, in my opinion, ought to be those activities that fall under our Category II--namely, those activities wherein the ECA serves as a facilitator of African interstate activities. Be it through feasibility studies, conference machinery, charter-writing, or supplying technical and economic assistance once operations have commenced, the ECA ought to clearly define its role as that of an agency that concerns itself with development activities that include more than one state. Undertaking activities which bring it into competition with the sectorially-specialized UN agencies, or even undertaking only inter-sectorial activities, does not provide a useful contribution, and hoping that the ECA will become the UN's operational arm for all its African activities is unrealistic. The ECA should not even concern itself with whether these activities will lead to regional cooperation or integration in the near future. It should simply reduce its range of activities--and in doing so, it might gain the advantage of making more clear to its clients what its function is as compared to other parts of the international aid machinery. The ECA's own concern that it ought to engage in 'action'programs (not just in studies) should be relieved not by competing with other agencies but by developing a more sharply-defined area of competence and by utilizing its resources for both study and programs in that limited area. Helping create an inter-state organization, and then providing it with the technical assistance it needs to carry out its designated function, is in fact a kind of 'action' program. It is the quality and relevance of the ECA's work that is really at issue, and for that quality and relevance to be enhanced, the range of its activities ought to be curtailed.

As more and more African inter-state institutions are created in Africa, the ECA may come to consider inter-state organizations its clients, rather than individual states. Many inter-state organizations fell apart in the 1960s because they were dependent on poor member-states for the human and financial resources to sustain themselves. The ECA's current efforts to sustain, and to develop a link with, the ECOWAS, indicates a promising direction for its energies.

Along with the ECA's decision to focus its energies on Category II activities should come the ability to help client-states draw up collective negotiating positions, and to follow through when the region tries to exert leverage within the international system in favor of a new economic order. If the ECA becomes a specialist in promoting regional activities on the African continent, it ought also to become a specialist in working out collective positions for promoting the interests of the region at negotiations pertaining to economic and social development. The ECA has had a tendency in the past to mirror international development thinking. Now it has the opportunity to emulate one aspect of the ECLA's self-defined role under Prebisch: to become a lobbyist for its region in the international system. It almost seems that events have conspired to offer the ECA a new role if it is willing to accept the opportunity. It is precisely because regionalism and collective African action have greater momentum in Africa than they have in the international system at large that the ECA has the chance to establish itself as a lobbyist for regional interests and to reflect, for the first time, Africa's self-identified needs rather than those identified by conventional international wisdom of the day. Ironically, the problem for Adedeji is almost the converse of that faced by

Prebisch in the 1950s and '60s. While Prebisch had to argue that regionalism required an NIEO, Adedeji has to argue that the NIEO makes little sense for Africa unless it accompanies regionalism. Prebisch captured the imagination of Latin Americans by making a case for the NIEO, and then convinced them that regionalism was essential to national and regional development. Adedeji is dealing with a clientele which already sees (or is coming to see) the wisdom of collective action and inter-state institution-building, but which needs to be convinced not to forfeit slowly-built inter-state arrangements for the promise of an NIEO. Adedeji and the ECA will enhance the credibility of their arguments if they are able to give concrete support to their clients, and thereby set themselves apart from those still espousing the empty rhetoric of African Unity, as well as from those who offer the convincing--and yet, for Africa, dangerous--hope that the NIEO is the light at the end of a long, dark tunnel.

Reform of the ECA is both timely and realistic right now, because the ECA's most useful work in the past has been in promoting regionalism, and regionalism has become a more realistic goal for Africa in the last few years. I do not underestimate either the obstacles to regionalism on the African continent or the ECA's failures to clarify its role and to set a higher standard for the quality of its work. African leaders, for understandable reasons, have easily fallen under the influence of those ideologies promising a quick fix; and African unity, regional integration, and the NIEO have all promised more than they can deliver. Many African leaders share with Americans a tendency to be pragmatic--and with it the tendency to discard an old model for the promise of a new one when the old has not delivered immediately all that it offered. The ECA itself is, as we have seen, a weak institution, because as a UN Regional Commission with a dual mandate its mission has never been structurally clear, and because as an African institution it has lacked the leadership and resolve to clarify its mission by itself. And yet the ECA is still uniquely placed and uniquely qualified to serve many of the current needs of its clients.

The argument in support of the ECA as an institution for promoting African regionalism rests, of course, on its current capacity and its future potential. The argument in support of continued use of regional arrangements on the African continent rests on the assumption that neither increased national self-reliance can by itself overcome the obstacles to development peculiar to Africa.

I see in fact a twofold purpose for encouraging regionalism on the African continent. First, because most African states are small and weak, regionalism provides a way for them to exert leverage on their own behalf in the international system. This advantage of regionalism is the one that is perhaps most frequently cited; so-called collective action (or collective bargaining) has in the past and will in the future be the <u>only</u> means most African states have to maximize their interests in international negotiations. In this context regionalism is an essential component of any NIEO that wishes to benefit African states. The second and less-frequently mentioned purpose for encouraging regionalism is in a way premised on the first. That is, if regionalism-as-collective-bargaining does win a more favorable position for Africa in the international economic system, then African inter-state cooperation will be essential to converting increased capital resources into economic and social development. The limited bilateral and multilateral resource transfers made so far have had disappointing effects precisely because capital was not applied in a meaningful way to local needs. Regional arrangements can become the means through which African states--who are well aware of the particularities of the African continent--can develop and share the human and infrastructural capacities without which greater availability of capital will again lead to disappointment.

It may be true that larger markets, communication grids, inter-state banking and currency mechanisms, and inter-state training and research can be used and abused by industrial societies with investments in Africa. However, a fear of this should not blind us to the fact that the very mechanism that may make it possible for industrial states to further exploit Africa may be the same one that makes it possible for African states to develop their own economies and gain more control over their own fates. The strongest argument for making regionalism a part of the NIEO, then, is the fact that inter-dependence among countries on the African continent is perhaps the only way in which the smaller states can reduce their dependence on the international system (old or new) and can avoid becoming dependent on the larger states (i.e., Nigeria). There are no easy or quick solutions for Africa's many social, economic or political problems, but the admittedly imperfect ECA with its admittedly imperfect ideas of regionalism ought not to be discarded prematurely in favor of new and equally imperfect models.

In the words of ECA's current Executive Secretary, "economic co-operation and development will come to naught unless they are based on a coherent and realistic regional structure. . . ."[30] The Economic Commission for Africa has played a moderately useful role in this regard in the past and it could well play a more significant role in the future.

NOTES

1. For a comparative look at the UN Regional Commissions, see Robert Gregg, "The UN Regional Commissions and Integration in the Underdeveloped Regions," International Organization, Vol. XX, No. 2, Spring, 1966, pp. 208-232.

2. ECLA's professional staff throughout the sixties ranged between 80 and 100. By mid 1960s ECA's professional staff exceeded that of ECLA. However, while ECLA's staff was predominantly Latin American, ECA's staff was predominantly expatriate until the 1970s.

3. Prebisch's analysis and prescriptions were carried by him to UNCTAD when he became head of UNCTAD and continued to be developed within the studies and documentations of UNCTAD. UNCTAD work in turn became a central component of the NIEO as manifested in the Economic Rights of Man and the Declarations emanating out of the Sixth and Seventh Special Sessions of the UN General Assembly.

4. During an interview with the author at ECA headquarters in Addis Ababa in April, 1966.

5. I spent the better part of March and April, 1966, at ECA headquarters in Addis Ababa, during which time I interviewed 80% of ECA's professional staff and familiarized myself with the documentation and projected work programs then available.

6. For discussions of Anglophone Francophone splits and the Yaounde Convention, see William Zartman, The Politics of Trade Negotiations between Africa and the European Economic Community: The Weak Confront the Strong, Princeton Univ. Press, 1971; Isebill V. Gruhn, "The Lome Convention: Inching Towards Interdependence," International Organization, Vol. 30, No. 2, Spring, 1976, pp. 243-248.

7. See for example UN E/CN.14/72, December 1960.

8. West Africa, 18 February 1967, p. 227.

9. For a general discussion of the OAU, including references to its role and function and that of ECA, see Michael Wolfers, Politics in the Organization of African Unity, London: Methuen and Co., and New York: Harper and Row, 1976.

10. See Isebill V. Gruhn, Funcationalism in African: Scientific and Technical Integration, Unpublished Ph.D thesis, University of California, Berkeley.

11. See Michael Wolfers, Politics in the Organization of African Unity, Op. cit., pp. 97-99. See also Berhanykin Andemicael, The OAU and the UN Institute for Training and Research, New York: African Publishing Co., 1976.

12. James Magee, "ECA and the Paradox of African Cooperation," International Conciliation, No. 580, November, 1970, p. 44.

13. Ibid., p. 45.

14. The ECA and Specialized Agencies joint operations at ECA, e.g., ECA/FAO Joint Division at ECA, came to augment rather than replace FAO's regional office for Africa which continued to be located in Accra Ghana.

15. The Special Session of the UN General Assembly in the Autumn, 1975 known as the Seventh Special Session, though preceded and followed by numerous conferences and declarations, is frequently cited the occasion when demands for a New International Economic Order NIEO was formalized. See GA resolution 3172 (XXVIII) and GA res 3343 (XXIX) GA 3201 (S-VI) and 3202 (S-VI) May 1, 1974, GA 3281 (XXIX) December 12, 1974.

16. The Conference on International Economic Cooperation met periodically in Paris in 1976 and 1977. Twenty-seven countries participated Nine countries representing the industrial North and 19 representing the LCD countries. These

conferences were frequently referred to as the North-South Dialogue.

17. Zdenek Cervenka, "Funeral in Paris," *Africa*, No. 71, July 1977, p. 55-57.

18. Interview with G.A. Lardner 3/24/76 at ECA Headquarters in Addis Ababa, Ethiopia.

19. *Op. cit.*: D. Rothchild, *Politics and Integration*; J. Nye, *Pan Africanism and East African Integration*; A. Jalloh, *Political Integration in French Speaking Africa*.

20. The Third Revision of this document emerged June 25, 1976, E/CN.14/ECO/90/Rev 3; however the footnotes are taken from the same document, Rev 2.

21. Ibid., ECO 90, p. IV.

22. *Ibid*.

23. *Ibid*., ECO 90, p. V.

24. *Ibid*., ECO 90, p. VI.

25. *Ibid*., ECO 90, p. 3.

26. *Ibid*., ECO 90, p. 6.

27. *Ibid*, p. 6.

28. *Ibid*., p. 13.

29. *West Africa*, 26 September 1977, p. 1987.

30. *Op. cit.*, Statement by Adedeji to the UN Ad Hoc Committee on Restructuring of the Economic and Social Sectors of the UN System, Feb. 26, 1976.

# Appendixes

## Appendix I
## SELECTED AFRICAN REGIONAL AND SUB-REGIONAL ORGANIZATIONS FOR COOPERATION AND INTEGRATION

A.D.B. - African Development Bank

Founded: 4 August 1963

Members: Independent black African states (any African country which has the status of an independent state may become a member).

Aim: Contribute to the economic development and social progress of its members individually and jointly to finance investment projects designed to make the economies of its members increasingly complementary and to bring about an orderly expansion of their foreign trade.

B.C.E.A.O. Banque Centrale des États de l'Afrique de l'Ouest

Founded: 1955

Members: Benin, Ivory Coast, Niger, Senegal, Togo, and Upper Volta.

Aim: Serve as a central issuing bank for the members of the West African Monetary Union.

B.E.A.C. - Banque des États de l'Afrique Centrale (Bank of African Central States)

Founded: 15 July 1955 (in 1959, it became the B.C.A.E.C. and in 1973, it changed to the B.E.A.C.-Bank of the States of Equatorial Africa and the Cameroons).

Members: Cameroon, Central African Empire, Chad, Congo, and Gabon.

Aim: Act as the exclusive issue house for notes and coins in circulation within member states.

B.O.A.D. - Banque Ouest-Africaine de Developpement

Founded: 1973

Members: Benin, Ivory Coast, Niger, Senegal, Togo, and Upper Volta.

Aim: Initiated by the West African Monetary Union to promote economic integration and balanced development among its members.

C.E.A.O. - Communauté Économique de l'Afrique de l'Ouest

Founded: May 1970.

Members: Ivory Coast, Mali, Mauritania, Niger, Senegal, and Upper Volta.

Aim: To serve as an organization of exchange for agricultural products and a special preferential system for industrial goods and to promote economic cooperation especially in industry and transportation - not intended to be a customs union.

C.P.L.M. - Comité Permanet Consultatif du Maghreb (Maghreb Permanent Consultative Committee)

Founded: 1 October 1964

Members: Algeria, Morocco, and Tunesia.

Aim: Act as a consultative and technical organ for the purpose of studying problems affecting economic cooperation and move toward the establishment of a Maghreb economic community.

E.A.C. - East African Community

Founded: 1967 (currently disbanded).

Members: Kenya, Tanzania, and Uganda.

Aim: Institute a legal framework to strengthen the East African Common Market and absorb the common services and research activities of the East African Common Services

Organization. Many of these common services date back to the 1920s - 1940s.

E.C.O.W.A.S. - Economic Community of West African States (C.E.D.E.A.O. - Communauté Économique des États de l'Afrique de l'Ouest)

Founded: 28 May 1975

Members: Benin, Gabon, Gambia, Ghana, Guinea, Guinea Bissau, Ivory Coast, Liberia, Mali, Mauritania, Niger, Nigeria, Senegal, Sierra Leone, Togo, and Upper Volta.

Aim: Establish a customs union among member states within a period of 15 years; foster economic cooperation and development; improve relations among member countries.

Entente - Conseil de l'Entente

Founded: 29 May 1959

Members: Benin, Ivory Coast, Niger, Togo, and Upper Volta.

Aim: Promote economic development in the region; assist in preparing specific projects; mobilize funds from other sources.

L.C.B.C. Lake Chad Basin Commission

Founded: 22 May 1964

Members: Cameroon, Chad, Niger, and Nigeria.

Aim: Promote and coordinate the rational and equitable utilization of the water resources of the Lake Chad Basin for development purposes.

Mano River Union

Founded: 3 October 1973

Members: Liberia and Sierra Leone

Aim: Establish a customs union.

Niger River Commission

Founded: 1963

Members: Benin, Cameroon, Chad, Guinea, Ivory Coast, Mali, Niger, Nigeria, and Upper Volta.

Aim: Navigation and general economic development.

O.A.U. - Organization for African Unity

Founded: 25 May 1963

Members: All independent African States (except for white-ruled South Africa, Rhodesia and Namibia).

Aim: Promote unity and development; defend the sovereign and territorial integrity of the members; promote international cooperation; harmonize members economic development.

O.C.A.M. - Organization Commune Africaine and Mauricienne

Founded: 27 June 1966

Members: Benin, Central African Empire, Gabon, Ivory Coast, Mauritius, Niger, Rwanda, Senegal, Togo, and Upper Volta.

Aim: To strengthen African and Malagasy cooperation and promote political, economic, social and technical development.

O.M.V.S. - Organization pour la Mise en Valeur du Fleuve Senegal (Organization for the Development of the Sengal River)

Founded: March 1972 (replacing the Organisation des États Riverains du Senegal).

Members: Mali, Mauritania, and Senegal.

Aim: Develop the Senegal River Basin and serve a range of economic and social development functions.

Southern African Customs Union

Founded: 11 December 1969 (replacing Customs Agreement of 1910).

Members: Botswana, Lesotho, South Africa and Swaziland.

Aim: Maintain the free interchange of goods between members and the application by them of the same tariffs and trade regulations to goods imported from third parties.

U.D.E.A.C. - L'Union Douanière et Économique de l'Afrique Centrale (Central African Customs and Economic Union)

Founded: 8 December 1964

Members: Cameroon, Central African Empire, Congo, and Gabon.

Aim: "The gradual and progressive establishment of a common market; the expansion of national markets through the removal of obstacles to inter-regional trade, the coordination of development programs for the different sectors of production and the adoption of a procedure for the fair distribution of industrial products;" the harmonization of development planning.

U.E.A.C. - Union des États de l'Afrique Centrale

Founded: 2 April 1963

Members: Chad, Zaire.

Aim: Create a customs union and coordinate social, technical and defense policies.

U.M.O.A. - Union Monétaire Ouest-Africaine (West African Monetary Union)

Founded: 12 May 1962 (new treaty signed 14 November 1974)

Members: Benin, Ivory Coast, Niger, Senegal, Togo, and Upper Volta.

Aim: Maintain a common currency whose issue was entrusted to the African financial community and is legal tender throughout the territory of the Union.

W.A.C.H. - West African Clearing House

Founded: 1976

Members: Benin, Ivory Coast, Niger, Senegal, Togo, and Upper Volta (the members of U.M.O.A.) and Gambia, Ghana, Liberia, Nigeria, and Sierra Leone.

Aim: Handle payments between the central banks of the member states in order to facilitate trade and financial transactions.

## Appendix 2
## MEMBER STATES OF THE UNITED NATIONS ECONOMIC COMMISSION FOR AFRICA

The 49 member States of the United Nations Economic Commission for Africa, with the dates on which they become members:

| Member | Date of Admission |
|---|---|
| Algeria | 8 October 1955 |
| Angola | 1 December 1976 |
| Benin | 20 September 1960 |
| Botswana | 17 October 1966 |
| Burundi | 18 September 1962 |
| Cape Verde | 16 September 1975 |
| Central African Empire | 20 September 1960 |
| Chad | 20 September 1960 |
| Comoros | 12 November 1975 |
| Congo | 20 September 1960 |
| Djibouti | 20 September 1977 |
| Egypt[1] | 24 October 1945 |
| Equatorial Guinea | 12 November 1968 |
| Ethiopia | 13 November 1945 |
| Gabon | 20 September 1960 |
| Gambia | 21 September 1965 |
| Ghana | 8 March 1957 |
| Guinea | 12 December 1958 |
| Guinea-Bissau | 17 September 1974 |
| Ivory Coast | 20 September 1960 |
| Kenya | 16 December 1963 |

1. Egypt and Syria were original Members of the United Nations from 24 October 1945. Following a plebiscite on 21 February 1958, the United Arab Republic was established by a union of Egypt and Syria and continued as a single Member. On 13 October 1961, Syria, having resumed its status as an independent State, resumed its separate membership in the United Nations.

| Member | Date of Admission |
|---|---|
| Lesotho | 17 October 1966 |
| Liberia | 2 November 1945 |
| Libya | 14 December 1955 |
| Madagascar | 20 September 1960 |
| Malawi | 1 December 1964 |
| Mali | 28 September 1960 |
| Mauritania | 27 October 1961 |
| Mauritius | 24 April 1968 |
| Morocco | 12 November 1956 |
| Mozambique | 16 September 1975 |
| Niger | 20 September 1960 |
| Nigeria | 7 October 1960 |
| Rwanda | 18 September 1962 |
| São Tomé and Príncipe | 16 September 1975 |
| Senegal | 28 September 1960 |
| Seychelles | 21 September 1976 |
| Sierre Leone | 27 September 1961 |
| Somalia | 20 September 1960 |
| Sudan | 12 November 1956 |
| Swaziland | 24 September 1968 |
| Togo | 20 September 1960 |
| Tunisia | 12 November 1956 |
| Uganda | 25 October 1962 |
| United Republic of Cameroon | 20 September 1960 |
| United Republic of Tanzania[1] | 14 December 1961 |
| Upper Volta | 20 September 1960 |
| Zaire | 20 September 1960 |
| Zambia | 1 December 1964 |

1. Tanganyika was a Member of the United Nations from 14 December 1961 and Zanzibar was a Member from 16 December 1963. Following the ratification on 26 April 1964 of Articles of Union between Tanganyika and Zanzibar, the United Republic of Tanganyika and Zanzibar continued as a single Member, changing its name to the United Republic of Tanzania on 1 November 1964.

Appendix III

ECA OPERATIONAL PROGRAMME 1979-1981 SECTORIAL DISTRIBUTION (United States Dollars)*

| | | Total | 1979 | 1980 | 1981 |
|---|---|---|---|---|---|
| 1. | Socio-economic research and planning | 98 132 | 98 132 | - | - |
| 2. | Agriculture | 1 189 990 | 273 202 | 477 988 | 429 800 |
| 3. | Industry | 1 053 075 | 593 177 | 344 098 | 115 800 |
| 4. | International trade and finance | 2 067 088 | 977 171 | 699 917 | 390 000 |
| 5. | Social development | 3 110 882 | 1 584 318 | 797 310 | 729 254 |
| 6. | Natural resources | 3 741 568 | 1 725 980 | 1 187 588 | 828 000 |
| 7. | Transport communications and tourism | 819 780 | 593 990 | 142 790 | 83 000 |
| 8. | Public administration management and manpower development | 5 075 885 | 1 724 885 | 1 631 250 | 1 719 750 |
| 9. | Statistics | 2 145 700 | 880 700 | 608 000 | 657 000 |
| 10. | Population | 2 116 900 | 748 900 | 615 000 | 753 000 |
| 11. | Economic cooperation | 2 965 432 | 1 045 132 | 945 000 | 966 300 |
| | Subtotal | 24 375 432 | 10 245 587 | 7 457 941 | 6 671 904 |
| | Programme support costs | 3 111 029 | 1 339 640 | 944 581 | 826 808 |
| | Total | 27 486 461 | 11 585 227 | 8 402 522 | 7 498 712 |
| | Support services | 3 349 350 | 1 032 350 | 1 114 400 | 1 202 600 |
| | Grand total | 30 835 811 | 12 617 577 | 9 516 922 | 8 701 312 |

*E/CN.14/709 p. 5.

## Appendix 4
## ECA-SPONSORED INSTITUTIONS AND THEIR LOCATIONS*

1. African Regional Organization for Standardization (ARSO): Ghana
2. Purchasing and Supplies Organization: Morocco
3. Association of African Trade Promotion Organization: Morocco
4. African Association of Cartography: Algeria
5. Union of African Railways: Zaire
6. Port Management Association of North Africa: Tunisia
7. Port Management Association for West and Central Africa: Zaire
8. East African Mineral Resources Development Centre: Tanzania
9. Regional Centre for Specialized Services in Surveying and Mapping: Kenya
10. Regional Centre for Training and Aerial Surveys: Nigeria
11. Association of African Central Banks: Ethiopia (ECA)
12. Trans-African Highways Authority/Bureau: Ethiopia (ECA)
13. Institute for Economic Development and Planning (IDEP): Senegal
14. African Development Bank (ADB): Ivory Coast
15. Economic Community for West African States (ECOWAS): Nigeria
16. West African Rice Development Association (WARDA): Liberia
17. Multinational Programming and Operational Centres (MULPOCs): Zambia, Cameroon, Niger, Morocco, Rwanda

*Not in order of establishment.

18. Regional Centres for Demographic Studies: Ghana, Cameroon, Egypt

19. Association of African Airlines: Kenya

20. Association for Social Work Education in Africa (ASWEA): Ethiopia

21. Association of African Financial Development Institutions: Ivory Coast

22. African Training and Research Centre in Administration (CAFRAD): Morocco

23. African Training and Research Centre for Women (ATROW): Ethiopia (ECA)

24. African Centre for Applied Research and Training in Social Development: Libya

INSTITUTIONS FOR WHICH LOCATIONS ARE NOT YET DETERMINED

1. Industrial Property Organization for English-speaking Africa
2. African Remote Sensing Council
3. Remote Sensing Centres (Egypt, Kenya, Nigeria, Upper Volta)
4. African Regional Centre for Technology
5. Pan-African Telecommunications Union

# Selected Bibliography

## Books


Anang-Dei, Michael. The Administration of Ghana's Foreign Relations. 1957-65. London: Athelone Press, 1975.

Andemiael, Berhaykin. The OAU and the U.N. Institute for Training and Research. New York: African Publishing Co., 1976.

Chrisman, Robert, Hare, Nathan, Eds. Pan Africanism. New York: Bobbs-Merrill Co., 1974.

Foltz, William. From French West Africa to the Mali Federation. New Haven: Yale University Press, 1965.

Geiss, Immanual. The Pan African Movement. New York: Africane Publishing Co., 1974.

Haq, Mahbub ul. The Poverty Curtain. New York: Columbia University Press, 1976.

Deutsch, Karl et. al. Political Community and the North Atlantic Area. Princeton, New Jersey: Princeton University Press, 1957.

Jalee, Pierre. The Third World in World Economy. New York: Monthly Review Press, 1969.

_________. The Pillage of the Third World. New York: Monthly Review Press, 1968.

Haas, Ernst B. The Uniting of Europe: Political, Social, and Economic Forces 1950-57. Stanford, California: Stanford University Press, 1958.

_________. Beyond the Nation State: Functionalism and International Organization. Stanford, California: Stanford University Press, 1964.

________. The Obsolescence of Regional Integration. Berkeley, California. Berkeley Institute of International Studies: University of California, 1975.

Green, Reginald, Seidman, Ann. Unity or Poverty?: The Economics of Pan Africanism. Baltimore, Maryland: Penguin Books, 1968.

Gruhn, Isebill V. "Functionalism in Africa: Scientific and Technical Cooperation." Unpublished Ph.D dissertation, University of California, Berkeley, 1967.

Jalloh, Abdul. "The Politics and Economics of Regional Political Integration in Central Africa." Unpublished Ph.D dissertation, University of California, Berkeley, 1969.

Legvold, Robert. Soviet Policy in West Africa. Cambridge, Massachusetts: Harvard University Press, 1975.

Legum, Colin. Pan Africanism: A Short Political Guide. New York: Praeger, 1962.

Nkrumah, Kwame. The Autobiography of Kwame Nkrumah. London: Thomas Nelson and Sons, 1957.

________. I Speak of Freedom. London: Heinemann, 1961.

________. Africa Must Unite. New York: Praeger, 1963.

Nye, Joseph S. Jr. Pan Africanism and East African Integration. Cambridge, Massachusetts: Harvard University Press, 1965.

Nyerere, Julius. Freedom and Socialism. Dar es Salaam: Oxford University Press, 1963.

Rothchild, Donald, ed. Politics of Integration, Nairobi: East Africa Publishing House, 1968.

Rothstein, Robert L. The Weak in the World of the Strong. New York: Columbia University Press, 1977.

Tinberg, Jan, ed. Reshaping the International Order: A Report to the Club of Rome. New York: E.P. Dutton & Co., 1976.

Wildavsky, Aaron. The Politics of the Budgetary Process. Boston: Little Brown & Co., 1964.

Wolfers, Michael. Politics in the Organization of African Unity. London: Methuen and Co., New York: Harper & Row, 1976.

Zartmann, William. The Politics of Trade Negotiations Between Africa and the European Economic Community. The Weak Confront the Strong. Princeton, New Jersey: Princeton University Press, 1971.

Articles

Gosovic, Branislav, Ruggie, John. "On the Creation of a New International Economic Order." Issue linkage and the Seventh Special Session of the U.N. General Assembly. International Organization, Vol. 30, No. 2 (Spring, 1976).

Gregg, Robert. "The U.N. Regional Commissions and Integration in the Underdeveloped Regions," International Organization, Vol. XX, No. 2 (Spring, 1966).

Gruhn, Isebill V. "Inching Towards Interdependence: The Lome Convention." International Organization, Vol. 30, No. 2 Spring, 1976).

Haas, Ernst B. and Schmitter, Philippe. "Economics and Differential Patterns of Integration: Projections about Unity in Latin America." International Organization, Vol. XVIII Autumn, 1964).

Magee, James. "ECA and the Paradox of Africa Cooperation." International Conciliation, No. 580 (November, 1970).

Nyerere, Julius. "A United States of Africa." Journal of Modern African Studies, Vol. 1, No. 1 (1963).

Schmitter, Philippe. "A Revised Theory of Regional Integration." International Organization, Vol. XXIV, No. 4 (1970).

________. "Further Notes on Operationalizing Some Variables Related to Regional Integration." International Organization, Vol. XXIII (Spring, 1969).

Shaw, Timothy. "The International Politics of Southern Africa." Issue, Vol. VII, No. 1 (Spring, 1977).

________. "The Political Economy of African International Relations." Issue, Vol. V, No. 4 (Winter, 1975).

Documents U.N. Economic Commission for Africa

E/CN. 14/424.
E/CN. 14/WP61 and M70-2480.
E/CN. 14/ECO/83.
E/CN. 14/INR/215.
E/CN. 14/649.
ECA Revised Medium Term Plan 1976-81.
ECN/TECO/31/Rev.
E/CN. 14/ECO. INV/34.
E/CN. 14/664.

ECA Press Release, ECA/1233 19 March 1976.
E/CN. 14/129.
E/CN. 14/STC/21.
E/CN. 14/STC/A Pur 1.
E/CN. 14/FISC/1.
E/CN. 14/AMA/16.
E/CN. 14/72 December 1960.
E/CN. 14/ECO/90/Rev. 2 and 3.
E/CN. 14/ECO/112.

U.N. Documents

Declaration and Action Program on The Establishment of a new International Economic Order. U.N. General Assembly Resolution 3201 (S-VI) and 3202 (S-VI) May 1, 1974.
Charter of Economic Rights and Duties of States, U.N. General Assembly Resolution 3281 (XXIX) December 12, 1974.
GA Official Records, Thirty-First Session Supplement No. 34 CA/31/34.
GA Resolution 3172 (XXVIII).
GA Report of the Ad Hoc Committee on the Restructuring of the Economic and Social Sector's of the United Nations System. 31 Session. Supplement 34 CA/31/34; Supplement 34B CA/31/34.

Journals

Africa
Africa Report
Afrique Nouvelle
International Organization
West Africa

# Index


Abas, Mekki, 103
Adedeji, Adebayo, 35-36, 130
African Development Bank, 68,81,119
African Regional Standards Organization, 80
Afro-Americans, 9-11
Anglophone, 31,70,105-106
Agriculture, 39

Bilateral Donors, 41-43
Boerma, A.H., 111

Cesaire, Aime, 9
Charter of Economic Rights and Duties of States, 22
Conference on International Economic Cooperation, see North-South Dialogue
Consultants, 52-53,77-78
Currency Clearing House, 82

Data, 69,75,105
Deutsch, Karl, 15-16

East African Community, 21
ECA, see Economic Commission for Africa
ECLA, see Economic Commission for Latin America
Economic Commission for Africa, Budget, 36-43; Dual Mandate, 44, 54,56,95,121; History, 1-4,103; Organizational Ideology, 35; Secretariat, 32; Staff, 31-34, 48-49, 58; Structure, 43-45, 54,57-58; Sub Regional Offices, 59-61,85, 91-92; Regional Centers, 47,75-76, 93,127; Work Program, 67
Economic Commission for Asia and the Far East, 1,110
Economic Commission for Europe, 1
Economic Commission for Latin America, 1,62, 68,100-103,108,110, 112,129
Economic Community of West African States, 68,84,92,119,127-128
Economic and Social Council, 1
ECO 90, 122-125
ECOWAS, see Economic Community of West African States
European Economic Community, 16,20

FAO, see Food and Agriculture Organization

Food and Agriculture Organization, 49,111
Francophone, 70,105-106, 111

Gardiner, Robert, 31-32, 58,62,68,103,110,113
General Assembly, 54
Ghana, 11

Haas, Ernst B., 14-15, 19,18-20
Houphouet-Boigny, Felix, 9

ILO, see International Labor Organization
Incrementalism, 18
Industrial Development, 45-54
Institution Building, 67, 78-85
Integration, see regional integration
Interdependence, 20
International Labor Organization, 72,76

Keita, Modibo, 12

Latin American Free Trade Association, 100
Lome Convention, 85

Mali Federation, 4,10
Manpower Training, 36, 71-77,123; Middle-level manpower training, 74,76
Mano River Union, 119, 127
Marxist Perspective, 16-17,24-26
MULPOCs, see Multinational Programming and Operations Centers
Multi-national Programming and Operations Centers, 60-62,87,90-93,95,127,128

Nationalism, 4
Negritude, 9-10
Neo-Colonialism, 16,19,25
Neo-Functionalism, 14-15, 18-19
New International Economic Order, 21-22, 24,72,96,99,113-122, 126,131
NIEO, see New International Economic Order
Nkrumah, Kwame, 3,9,11-13,16
North-South Dialogue, 23,114,115
Nyerere, Julius, 9,12

Organization of African Unity, 31-32,107-109, 112
Organization of American States,102
OPEC, 21

Padmore, George, 11
Pan-Africanism, 11-13
Prebisch, Raul, 32,62, 101,103,113,129-130

Research Centers, 92-94
Regional Center for Training in Aerial Survey, 93
Regional Cooperation, 13-14,117,125
Regional Womens Center, 94
Regional Integration, 14, 117,120

Revised Medium-term Plan 1976-81, 49-50, 93

Scandinavian Countries, 42
Science and Technology, 108
Second UN Development Decade, 21
Self-Reliance, 118-119, 125
Senghor, Leopold, 9-10
Seventh Special Session, 22
Sixth Special Session, 22
Statistics, 69,123

Technicial Assistance, 41-42
Telli, Diallo, 32,108
Transactionalists, 15-16

UNCTAD, see United Nations Conference on Trade and Development, 22,100
UNDATs, see United Nations International Multidisciplinary Development Advisory Teams
UNDP, see United Nations Development Program
UNESCO, 70,72,76
UNIDO, 48-49
United Nations Development Program, 21
United Nations International Multidisciplinary Development Advisory Teams, 59-60,87-90
UN Specialized Agencies, see separate agencies

West African Currency Clearing House, 68, 83-84
Workshops and Seminars, 71-77

Yaounde Agreements, 105